REFLECTIONS OF A
SELF FULFILLING PROPHECY

Dr. Eboni K. Wilson

REFLECTIONS OF A SELF FULFILLING PROPHECY
Copyright© 2010 by Dr. Eboni K. Wilson

Printed in the United States of America. All rights reserved under International Copyright Law. Contents and/or cover may not be reproduced in whole or part in any form without the expressed written consent of Dr. Eboni Wilson. {D.C.W.}

Photos Copyright Jovanka Novakovic | bauwerks.com

Graphic Design and Layout - EastGate Media

Published by:
Beautiful Visions Publication

ISBN 10-0615368891
ISBN 13-978-0-615-36889-4

Self Fulfilling Prophecy

Positive or negative expectations about situations, events, or people that may affect ones behaviors (consciously or unconsciously) to where they create circumstances in which those expectations end up becoming true.

Merton, R. K. (1968). Social Theory and Social Structure. New York, NY: Free Press.

Dedication

This book is dedicated to my brother Bernard Bennie Wilson, his influence on me is immeasurable. I work hard to make him proud every day. This book is also dedicated to the young, innocent kids in the ghetto; who, unfortunately, continue living blind and in poverty. This book is for the children who are suffering, as I once did, and for the individuals who need a lens to see into the world of a ghetto child.

Acknowledgement

I first want to thank the God who created us all; the God who is the good in everyone; the God who lacks the feeling of hate in his heart; the God who looks at life as precious no matter what a person's skin color is; the God who gave me the vision and the understanding of how our world works; the God who gave me the tenacity to change the miserable conditions that innocent kids live through every day; the God of love.

I want to acknowledge those who have helped me journey on my path to where I step each day and where I will step tomorrow. I would like to thank my high school coaches who helped "put me on the market" for college scouts to recognize my gift. Coach Johnson you helped me see another side of life – how it operates and the rules for functioning within it. Coach Chapel you helped me see how mainstream society functions. You opened up the weight room for me every day at six o'clock in the morning; I needed that release before my day began. I want to thank Jon Douglas for giving me a job outside of my community. You helped me understand that there is another life outside of the 'hood. Although you did not know it at the time, you changed the way I viewed society and life in general. You helped my ambitions grow into something other than what I saw every day.

BIRDS OF A FEATHER FLOCK TOGETHER

A place of birth, where my soul is cursed, along with a preconceived destiny, which is lying face up in a hearse
It's a shame how I've been trained not to use my brain, in a society consumed with pain
The black rain leaves unwanted stains in this manifestation, which contains an overload of crack and cocaine
So through this training process my life is bombarded with stress
Now I must confess, my heart is consumed with unhappiness, because everywhere I go I have to pray that I don't get shot in the chest
Do you see the bitterness, or do you choose to ignore
Come walk with me through this war and witness how many of our young babies lie dead on the floor.
We are poor and don't anyone adore our beautiful black faces, so what are we living for
We are created out of habit, breed like rabbits, stuck in a paradox, filled with panic
So now we run frantic for our lives, ducking and dodging bullets, searching for places to hide
This is how we are created, and unfortunately this is why we are hated, segregated and perpetuated as illiterate
You see, they premeditated, manifested, and invested in our downfall
It was driven by hatred, mixed in with faceless racist, who wanted to see us trapped in these places
Combined with no one who is considerate of our existence
So without persistence, we continue to have an empty conscience, Because we know that no one wants us
So without a fuss, we accept the crust of life and convince

ourselves that it's right
This is one of the reasons why we won't unite
Because despite all of the hidden opportunities, we can't even contemplate the idea of unity
We are too busy focused on the now, that the later refuses to consume our thoughts
It's because we bought into the created thought
Well, if you didn't catch the lesson, it is now about to be reiterated
They premeditated, manifested, and invested in our downfall
It was driven by hatred, mixed in with faceless racist, who wanted to see us trapped in unhappiness
Along with a psychological plantation, caging us from our destination, with this ongoing infiltration
I said with this ongoing infiltration we are consumed with anger and frustration, so please embrace this education, because it will soon spark your imagination
For right now, our minds are in retention, not to mention the severity of our prosperity
Now I hope I have delivered this message with clarity because rarely do I get a chance to open the minds of others
Others meaning my sisters and brothers
So in ending the word, I hope you set your mind free because for far too long it's been caged like a bird
Don't give up the fight, because we will unite and go on believing that tomorrow will be bright
Just don't give in because our world is consumed with sin, because as long as I'm breathing, you'll always have a friend.

Chapter One

1

Bernard wanted to be an electrical engineer...

It didn't take me long to realize this is not how things were supposed to be, because relative to everyone else around me my situation always seemed worse. Soon after this realization I knew, one thing... I'm different. I once heard May Angelou say, "we do the best that we can with what we know and when we know more, we will do better." Growing up I did just as Ms. Angelou said... the best I could with what I knew, which wasn't much. It's easy to hear about poverty when they talk about it in the paper or when you hear the latest statistic in the news, but it's different when it's your neighbors, friends, family but more importantly your own mother.

In my mind my family was supposed to be grounded by a strong black woman. You know, the type that held down her job, came home cooked, cleaned, and at the end of the day read a book and tucked you in at night, doing it all with a smile and a strong attitude that no one will mess with what's hers. Well, that's not quite what I had in Mama. I have to believe that in her mind Mama wanted the best for her family, but just did not have the right tools to be able to be a strong black woman, let alone a mother.

There were four boys in my family: Peanut was three years older than me, then Bernard who was two years older, me and Travie who was two years younger. My parents separated when I was three so my father, Benny as I affectionately call him, was in my life like a bad cold... here one day gone the next, never really knowing if and when he was going to return again. Because my mother had her focus on other endeavors, each of us did our own thing, when we wanted and how we wanted. We rarely celebrated holidays, birthdays, awards or achievements. The closest thing we got to a celebration was on the first and the fifteenth when the check from the government came. Mama would yearn for the checks, standing by the mailbox waiting the arrival of her thin green envelope, showing me one thing... to many, poverty is a mentality.

Neither of my parents graduated from high school, both working on again, off again minimum wage jobs. But ultimately instead of persevering, they always went back to the steady twice a month skinny green envelope the government provided. My mother was satisfied with life in the ghetto; her life on welfare was a lot easier than work. The little money we did have, I could not tell you where it went. My mother rarely paid the bills and we lived in the dark because we often did not have lights. We never had food, being forced to make pancakes out of flour and water and when we did have the luxury of milk, it was in powder form. Many nights we were forced to make our meals out of what ever was in the kitchen that was not moldy and at times we even had to use that. Mama didn't seem to care, her focus was somewhere else.

Benny was tall in stature, but beyond that I did not really know what type of man he was except that, according to Mama, he was a "no good bastard." I truly did not know what that meant, but I did know that it must not have been good, because the tone she said it in scared me. She often yelled other bad words at Benny, telling him not to come around, but when he was around, I felt more secure. I never got the feeling that Mama loved him or that he loved her because he did what he had to do and rarely did it include her or us. Mama often said he was not doing his part in raising us and that she had to pick up the slack. I guess this conflict is why Benny was never around.

Peanut concentrated all his time and energy on his gang family. I guess they showed him more love and affection than Mama did. This choice was one Peanut made early in life and no one could convince him that anything else would be better. He was a member of N.H.B; a neighborhood gang associated with the Bloods and started committing crimes when I was young. The gang, in his words, provided him with love, friendship, food and money, the necessities Mama and Benny weren't providing. In his world our life and community was like living in prison, so the consequences for his actions could not be any worse than what he was experiencing on a day-to-day basis. Peanut was conditioned to adapt to his environment for survival, losing his excitement for school, education and an opportunity to escape the ghetto. I thought, as a little brother looking up to him, that he gave up on leading the way for us way to prematurely.

Bernard, like Peanut, fell into the temptations of the neighborhood. He joined the HollyHood Piru, a gang associated with the Bloods. Out of all my brothers, Bernard was the one I looked up to the most. We looked alike; both loved 2Pac and bonded through the struggles Mama exposed us to. Bernard wanted to be an electrical engineer, but soon, instead of going to school, he collaborated with Peanut in plotting crimes and executing their plans. I was sad when I saw Bernard go down this road because I just knew he was going to pave the way for me. Bernard was around more than Peanut. To me, despite his deviant actions he was more like what a big brother should have been.

Travie was the socialite. He was always too caught up in being the center of attention to get into trouble. Being the youngest, he was spoiled and thought everything in life should be given to him with little, if any, work involved. He thought everything was owed to him and those around him should cater to his every need. With this attitude came his comedy. He was short, dumpy little dude, always searching for something funny, silly or outrageous to talk about. His presence just made you laugh and in our house that's what we needed sometimes.

Then there was me... I, as I said before, was always different. People always thought I was older than I really was because my size often dominated my appearance. Out of the four of us, I was the loner. I was much more content being by myself away from the destruction around me, free to dream of a world where comfort was reality and money came from hard work, not some green envelope twice a month. I can remember at about five years, really beginning to understand what was going on around me and within my family. From then on I knew, for kids in the 'hood, dreaming was never the problem; it was learning how to reach those dreams that tangled everything up.

Chapter Two

2

I could not believe what was about to transpire

Being five years old I often did not realize what was happening around me, but I knew the dynamics between my mother and uncle, Junior, as we knew him, were not ideal. In Grandma's two bedroom apartment there was me, Travie, Bernard, Peanut, Mama, Junior, his wife Shawn, their daughter Winter and Grandma. We got the luxury, if that's what you would call it, of living in one room together. No one had a job but they utilized the federal government to help Grandma pay the rent. The selfishness in them knew that she would never kick them out and that they could use her for any and everything they could. This situation seemed to put a lot of stress on Grandma, but they did not care, it was all about them.

Grandma was a fragile woman, who did not keep herself up. She was old and suffered from severe arthritis and soon was diagnosed with cancer. Struggling with her health she could not afford the burdens of her children's lives, but did as much as she could for the sake of us. Her unselfishness was a breath of fresh air to me, since everyone else was strictly self centered. To me life at Grandma's was always filled with some type of drama or situation. I used to sit next to her rocking chair and talk with her about absolutely nothing, but it made me feel like she was invested in me and wanted me to be happy.

One day when sitting next to her oversized rocking chair, she started to move around, searching her chair and pockets. I gently asked,
"Grandma, what's wrong? Did you lose something? Can I help?" She continued to squirm and eventually stood up, looking at her seat in bewilderment. She indicated that she was missing a large sum of money. Her face told it all. I had never seen her really mad, but I knew she had it in her. Her face was red, her breathing was hard and her body seemed to tremble with anger. I was petrified that she would kick out who ever stole from her, so I was glad it was not me. Mama was gone, so I assumed our family would have a roof to sleep under for another night. Grandma immediately confronted Junior and Shawn. I knew what was next… or at least I thought I knew.

In my mind, they were going to deny it and eventually confess giving her back some of the money, knowing they probably had already used the funds for something illegal. I watched Grandma tell them to give her the money back politely, while Junior and Shawn got loud, completely denying stealing from her. After a few requests and the conversation getting louder and louder, then next thing I knew, Grandma had pulled a shiny gun from under her rocking chair. I could not believe what was about to transpire. Junior and Shawn did not acknowledge the gun, nor care that she had drawn a weapon. They continued to rant and rave that they did not take her money. All I could think about was the rule I was always told from when I was a young boy... if you pull a gun be sure that you were prepared to use it. Grandma was prepared.

"If my money is not returned to me this instant, I will shoot and I will shoot to kill your ass." I guess Grandma already knew that rule. Junior and Shawn must not have thought Grandma was serious. They continued to deny the theft and jokingly egged her on. Grandma then said,

"Don't patronize me." The next thing I knew, she had rose to her feet with the help of her rusted out cane and rounds of bullets were coming out the barrel of a .38-caliber pistol. I could smell the rounds fired; it was like something burning in the house. I watched bullets fly through the house, seemingly whistling by my head, I heard the sound of panic as Junior and Shawn ran to the back of the house, barely escaping the flight of the bullets. I was in shock. I did not move. I just stood frozen in time, it seemed like slow motion. All I could think was what was I supposed to do? What do I say? Do I hide? Will Grandma really shoot them? Will I get caught in the cross fire? Should I hide? But before I completed my thoughts, it was quiet.

After she ran out of bullets, Grandma, slowly sat back down, asked me if I was alright, placed the 38 down and started to rock in her rocking chair. Still in shock, I looked around to appraise the damage. I knew Junior and Shawn were not hit, but was there anyone else hurt? Where did the rounds go? Who will clean the mess up? While assessing the damage, I noticed a bullet had gone straight though the kitchen cabinet, through a jar of cream, through the wall and out the house. It was while I was looking around the house that I came to two conclusions:

1) Don't mess with Grandma or her money
2) Junior and Shawn got what they deserved!

※

While living with Grandma I learned pretty early on that Junior and I did not get along. Most of the time I wished we did not live with, or near, him. If Junior was not around things might have been a little bit easier to handle. His appearance was solely based upon his dependence on drugs. When he was heavily addicted to crack he was skinny, almost frail, and when not using he was a nice full-sized man who apparently had a lot of charisma. He was not much of a man. I often looked at him as someone my age. He reminded me of the neighborhood punk: the one who bullied those around him to make themselves seem powerful. In actuality he was weak. He knew how to push my buttons and frequently got under my skin. He never wanted me or anyone in my family to be successful or have any taste of positivity. If he could, he would sabotage those experiences for his own enjoyment. When first moving with Grandma, he talked to me like I was dumb, just to see if he could infuriate me. He would send me on errands into dangerous situations sometimes at night, or without supervision, just because he knew he could and I had no choice but to obey him.

Under his supervision we had the freedom to do what we wanted, he was always high and drunk, and so as long as I stayed out of his festivities, I was fine. One day, we were in the backyard and he was drunk as a skunk and partaking in his drug of choice for that moment – weed. My brothers and I were playing tag and ignoring him. "Come here," he demanded. As we stopped playing, I did not know what to expect… was he sending us out into the neighborhood, was he going to try to make me angry, or was he going to humiliate us in front of his friends. He then said,

"Drink this and smoke this." I did not know what the drink was and it could not be that bad, because he drank it all the time. I also saw other family members, including Mama, having some so I believed it must not be harmful or bad for me.

As I took the cup from his hand, I sniffed it to find that it smelled like the stuff Mama put on my cuts when they were bleeding. But I thought that smell does not always mean that it will taste bad, so I decided to have a go for it. I took a big gulp.... The burn, it was excruciating. I felt as though my chest was going to explode. It was awful. I have never felt something so awful on my insides. Why in the world would anyone do that to their body? Who likes that feeling? I knew right then and there I was not going to have any more, nor was I going to smoke whatever he was smoking. Peanut and Bernard took sips, smiled and laughed at me and my reaction. Did they like it? How? They then took a hit of the weed, which looked like a hand-made cigarette. They smiled again. The next thing I knew they were participating in the merriment with Junior. I was amazed, not because I understood what had transpired, but because they could stand the taste of that horrible stuff. Soon after, they started regularly hanging out with Junior to sip and smoke. Junior had just introduced them to a life I never, ever wanted to experience again. I knew that what they were doing was wrong, I hope they did too, but because they were actively engaging in sipping and smoking, they probably didn't. I think they thought they were cool. But to me, cool was simple, do not get involved and stay away from Junior. He's no good, period.

YOUR DISCIPLINE

You chastise me, but out of spite.

Instead of spanking me, you punch me, as if you want to fight.

I'm only nine years old,

But you are my guardian so I'll do as I'm told,

You don't have to beat me with your fist just because this is your version of how to scold.

How cold, if you keep it up, I won't grow old.

I remember you pushing me on the dirt, kicking me while I was down, you simpleton jerk

I hated your guts.

I prayed every night that God send somebody to come and kick your butt.

You treated me like trash,

You smacked me upside my head. Only because I passed.

What did I ever do to you to deserve this treatment?

Couldn't you see that I was looking for somebody to talk to, so I could vent,

But you were too immature to ask me why I did the things I did.

You let your anger get the best of you, so you slapped a little kid.

hated the slum I was in

And I prayed to God to ask him why I couldn't be in a family like Phil Drumin's

I guess it's different strokes for different folks, so I'm stuck here with you,

Your discipline, your anger, and your can of brew.

You're not my dad, you know who brought this pain that's so hard,

Yet this is your way of discipline, unaware that you've scarred

But it's cool, I'm grown and I prayed for this day for so long,

And now I am finally on my own

With my destiny in my hand.

Now I can learn from your mistakes and become a real man.

I wrote this, only with the intent to vent,

I needed to release my anger, so that I could circumvent.

With this release I end in peace.

Pain from the heart that now can cease.

Chapter Three

3

This was my new found way to get what I needed

At an early age, I figured out that if I stayed out of everyone's way and minded my business, I should be fine. I often wanted to escape and leave the controlling, drug addicted, gang banging, back stabbing adults my world was consumed with. Often times I had nowhere to go, until I figured out that I could escape the madness of gangs, drugs and foolish adults at school.

By the time I was six, my life was so crazy that school was always an afterthought. I did not complete homework, nor was school a priority to my family. I guess coming from individuals who never finished high school, it was pointless to attend and move forward with something that was never going to really matter anyway. I thought different. Though my miserable existence did not change outside the school house, from 8:00 AM to 4:00 PM, I had the freedom to explore new thoughts, learn new skills and develop a new mindset for how I was going to be when I was old enough to make my own choices.

Because life at home was never consistent I started pumping gas to get money to eat. It was not the best living, but pumping eight tanks for a quarter each was enough to feed me at the local burger shop across the street (experiencing my first taste of burgers and fries, which was far better than rice, beans or flour and water pancakes). This was my new found way to get what I needed without depending on "them." The joy of this, so-called career, was that it did not interfere with school. Knowing that I was safe at school, I never missed a day and then I could leave and pump gas for a few hours, eat and go home before the street lights came on. What a perfect set up.

As I got deeper into the gas pumping business, I developed some rules to live by to ensure my career would continue to flourish:

1) I could never let Mama or anyone else know. Mama would steal my money or tell me to stop. Everyone else would be mad or sabotage my career.

2) I had to be home before dark. The streets of South Central were never safe, especially after night fall.

3) Never let the gas attendant see me pumping gas. If they did they would kick me off the lot and I would not be able to eat.

4) Always have a story to tell the driver... it was my birthday and I needed spare change to eat, I had not ate that day and needed change, or a simple request to pump gas for a quarter usually worked fine.

On most nights I did not have the chance to do my homework. But I didn't care I was making money and to me there was nothing better than that. Soon I learned to branch out in my money earning business. I started washing cars, helping people with their groceries and sometimes just flat out begged. With the money I was earning I not only got to eat, but started buying clothes and toys, but most importantly I kept my sanity. I did what I had to do to survive, both physically and mentally and I started to fully understand the power of money and the value of a dollar.

I continued to put more distance between myself and my family, leaving early enough to get to school to have two helpings of breakfast, sit in class and daydream about work after school, leave right when the bell rang, because daylight was a necessity in my career, make my money, maybe shop, always eat then make it home to get in the bed. Weekends were even better... dawn to dusk was full of hard work to get good meals. One day I even tried to introduce Bernard to the career; I thought I could trust him. The day he came to see what I did we made a whole four dollars and ninety-five cents. That was the best I had ever done. We ate burgers and fries and I showed him my life of sanity away from home. He was not convinced, and even went and told Grandma of the work I had been pursuing. She was not happy and told me that I had to stop immediately. Rule one broken.

The joy was that though I told them I had stopped, they were so self-absorbed they did not notice that I was still gone all day doing what I had to do. It was unfathomable in my mind to sit in that house and listen to them complain about everything as well as me continuing to be the target of Junior's cruel jokes and anger. As the year went on I continued to go to school every morning and go to work in the afternoon. My career was jump started;

I was averaging two dollars and twenty five cents during the week and upwards of four dollars on the weekend. In my mind, I was living the good life, but little did I know what was about to happen...

Chapter Four

4

"If you hate me then I am going to kill myself..."

Being eight was great. I was old enough to be on my own, my business was flourishing and living with Grandma was not too bad. Junior pretty much left me alone, I was growing bigger and stronger, Peanut was barely around and I was disappointed in Bernard for telling Grandma about my business venture, but overall I was maintaining.

School was fine, my grades were poor, but I did not care, I was making money. I started saving and had accumulated a large sum, still being able to eat and every once in a while, buy myself the most wanted pleasure of childhood, candy. As I collected my money I knew I could not carry it all on me, for fear of being robbed. On the flip side, I knew if I left my money in the house, Mama might find it and steal it. I decided that my best bet would be to keep it with me at all times and take the risk of being robbed.

If I was robbed at least it would be by a stranger and not my family. Furthermore, if that happened I might be able to remember their face and find them later and have Peanut and Bernard beat them up.

As my money built up I became very excited and nervous. Having collected over fifty dollars, I was very cautious of who saw me with my money, what I did when I got home and where I put my money at bed time. Over the weeks my money continued to grow and before I knew it I had over a hundred dollars: one hundred, seven dollars and seventy nine cents to be exact. I was proud of my hard work. When I got home that night, I acted as usual knowing the next day, being Friday, I was going to be able to make even more... I anticipated my wad of cash being so big, it would bulge out of my pocket. I just had to hide it until the morning. When no one was around I slipped the bills out of my pocket and knew that pushing the money in my shoe, way to the top of the toe, was the best place to put it. No one would ever find it there.

As I lay down all I could do was dream of the next day and my wad of money in my shoe. That shoe was all I had and was going to allow me to get a lot of things I had never had before. The next morning I awoke to silence in the house. That was a rarity with all of us under one roof. I looked out the window to see light barely peering through the homes. GREAT! I could get dressed, get my money and make it to school and then to the gas station without having to talk to anyone. I ran to my shoe, reached up to the toe and found nothing but four pennies. I knew I had put it in that shoe. I reached again, nothing. I crawled under the bed to find the other shoe, reached in nothing. This was impossible. Who knew that was where I put my money? Why would someone steal from me? All that hard work down the drain. Peanut? Bernard? It could not be either of them 'cause they were making their own money husslin'. The only one who could have done it was Mama.

I had to find her. I waited. She was not at home, but she would be back. As I waited I started to get angry, as time went on I became more and more infuriated. I wanted to punch her in her face. She was not supposed to steal from me, her son. She better have a good reason. When she came in the door, I immediately confronted her,
"Did you steal my money?" She acted as if she did not hear me, which made it even worse,
"DID YOU STEAL MY MONEY?" She looked at me, with a glazed look on her face and said,
"Finders keepers." I looked at her with rage and said,
"I hate you."

Her reaction to my anger made me feel guilty, though she was the one who did wrong. Her eyes flooded with tears and she said,
"If you hate me then I am going to kill myself, then you won't have to worry about me stealing from you anymore." She then went into the bathroom hysterical, found a bottle of pills, poured a handful into hand and pressed them right into her mouth. Bernard grabbed the bottle and I grabbed her throat so she couldn't swallow. Together we struggled against Mama and managed to get her to spit the pills out. She continued to bawl like a newborn baby. We comforted her as she slowly relaxed. We walked her to the bed and continued to comfort her until she fell asleep.

We did not go to school that day for fear she might try and harm herself. How could Mama stealing money from me turn into my fault and make me feel so horrible? The next day Mama and I talked. I told her I loved her but stealing from me was not what she was supposed to do. She agreed and told me it would never happen again.

                                                  ≈•≈

    Now that Mama and I had an understanding things were getting back to how they were before the theft. I was making my money and people left me alone. School was a different story. Though I was attending, my grades continued to suffer and instead of asking for help, I would get angry and act out. There were numerous occasions where my behavior caused me to get kicked out of class or suspended. But I did not care 'cause I had a job and I was making money. I continued to come to school early to eat a large breakfast often trying to sneak into the line two or three times to get more food.

    Soon the cafeteria personal noticed I was always the first one there in the morning and ate more than once, so they made a deal with me. If I came in and helped them prepare the food, they would give me extra helpings and the leftovers from lunch. As I thought about it this was a good deal. I was already coming early, I was hungry and it did not interfere with my after school job. So I started immediately. I helped clean, chop and mix. It was not too bad. They would not let me actually cook, so when it was time for them to prepare, I would go in the back of the cafeteria through the door to the auditorium and sit at the piano until it was time to eat.

    As time went on, I started picking up bit-by-bit, piece-by-piece how to play the piano. Before I knew it I had learned Chariots of Fire by ear. As I improved the cafeteria ladies would encourage me, applaud me and tell me how beautiful the music sounded. I did not believe them because the only thing I was good at was being alone and making money. But I continued to play to get my food. A perfect deal.

~•~

Living at Grandma's was still convenient for all involved. She let us move into the garage for more room. This was good in my eyes because then I did not have to come in direct contact with Junior, though he was always lurking somewhere. Mama had a boyfriend, who was not the friendliest of people and did not treat us nice. He often would shoe us along or yell at us to get away, so I did not say much to him. What I did not know was that he was beating on Mama. She would come home with black eyes and bruises, never really letting us know where they came from, but Peanut and Bernard had their suspicions.

I guess one day Mama had had enough. She told him she no longer wanted to be his girlfriend, that she was leaving him and that he was never to return to our house. The conversation quickly got heated and I could not make out what they were saying except a bunch of really bad words. The argument seemed to go on forever, but eventually he stormed away in pure anger.

Later that night while we were sleeping, I awoke to Mama frantically screaming and crying. I smelled a strong odor of something burning. I looked at Mama and there was unadulterated terror in her eyes. Her boyfriend had come back and set the garage on fire. As I looked at the door it was engulfed in flames. The smoke got thick and my eyes began to water. I could hear the crackling of the flames and the timbers slowly deteriorating with the blaze. The heat from the inferno was like nothing I had ever felt before. We had to get out.

I ran to the front and tried to push the door open, but it was blocked. The man had caged us in. Was this it? Was I about to die at the hands of a man who was so angry at Mama he was willing to take her and her children's lives? We all started crying out for help as loud as we could. I can hear Mama's voice, "We can't find a way out!" I heard Peanut yell, "Help!" We all tried to collectively push the door... Nothing. My eyes were burning. There was black smoke everywhere, and I could barely see Mama, Peanut, Bernard or Travie. The flames got closer; I could almost reach out and touch them. We were huddled in the garage with no way out, the fire was getting bigger and bigger and we were about to die.

As the fire progressed, I could not cry, try to get out or move. It was a surreal moment and there was nothing I could do about it, but know that this was the end of a miserable life, and I was about to experience true happiness. Then I heard a loud bang. The door opened and there were three neighbors standing in the glow of the flames. They heard our cries for help and moved the blockade just in time. We all ran out of the garage making it just before the large support beam in the middle of the building fell to the ground. As we stood there and watched the garage, our home, burn down I could only think that that night I was supposed to die and barely escaped. The fire department soon arrived and sprayed down Grandma's house, so the flames would not catch to her home. The garage burned to the ground with all of our belongings and the next thought that came to my head was: where were we going to live?

Chapter Five

5

"You don't know what you just did..."

In the days following the fire Grandma allowed us to stay with her again. Soon after Mama spoke with some county officials about the situation, her ex was locked up, and she let us know we would be moving into our own place. This was the best news ever. We could start over, fresh: no more fighting, no more Junior, no more cramped quarters and at last space where we could call ourselves a real family. So that weekend we packed up the few items we could salvage from the fire and headed around town to the new apartment.

The new place was fantastic. It was a three bedroom with all the amenities. We had heat, air, a color TV and even bedrooms with windows. Mama had her own room, Peanut and Bernard shared a room while Travie and I were roommates, we also had a living room, dining room and a kitchen with a new refrigerator.

There was still the looming issue of how we were going to eat every night, but I didn't care we were living in the lap of luxury as far as I was concerned. I still had my cafeteria work at school (though the travel was going to be a little further), my career at the gas station in the afternoon and I seemingly had found a new friend from around the block, Marcos.

Marcos and his family were what I always dreamed I wanted my family to be. Both of his parents worked hard. His father was a laborer who, after dinner, went back to work a second shift, while his Mother worked as a nurse during the day. Despite their grueling hours, every time I was at Marcos's they all ate as a family. Being with Marcos was fun. He had a Nintendo, which allowed me to be the master of Super Mario Brothers. He helped me with at least trying to do my homework and he was a friend I could bond with like a brother. On days when it rained and I could not go to the gas station Marcos would invite me over and we would play Nintendo, watch TV and have a snack. Then he would do homework, while I pretended to work, but I actually was daydreaming about living like Marcos all the time. I never saw them fight, yell or talk down to each other. They seemed perfect, like the Mexican version of the Cosby's.

One day, while walking home we encountered a group of three boys. I had no idea who they were because I had not been around the neighborhood that much, but Marcos immediately told me that we had to head the other way because they wanted to beat him up. I asked why they wanted to beat him up, but Marcos just kept insisting that we had to turn around. I told Marcos that was not an option and that I was not going to let anyone hurt him. As we got closer to the three boys, who could not have been more than two years older than us, Marcos began to tremble. I knew he wanted to cry, but was holding back his tears with all his might. I'm sure in his mind he was about to get pounded by these boys while I watched. When we got close enough, Marcos stopped as if he had lead in his shoes. I continued to walk right up to the boys and approached the biggest one, who I assumed was the leader.

"Leave Marcos alone." I stated in a firm and intimidating voice. The leader looked at me and disregarded my statement by calling Marcos a name and making fun of his clothing. He then went up to Marcos and demanded his money. Marcos stepped back, turned and ran like the wind. I was left there with the three boys looking at me. The second boy said,

"Now what are you going to do? It seems as though your little buddy left you all alone." I told him Marcos had nothing to do with this anymore because I told them to stop messing with him. The boys laughed. I indicated that if they wanted to do something about it they should meet me behind the building.

As we moved to the back of the building, the boys taunted me and acted as if they were big, bad and hard. When we arrived at the back of the building, the leader shouted,

"What are you going to do? Hit me?" Instead of replying, I cocked my arm back and hit him so hard he fell to the ground with blood running out of his nose and mouth. He was in shock. The other two boys stood there in disbelief and backed away almost running home. The leader looked at me and said,
"You don't know what you just did. I'm gonna get my brother and then you will be dead." I looked at him as though I had daggers coming out my eyes and said,
"I don't care go get him... I'll be waiting right here." He slowly stood up and ran to his home, which was around the corner.

About five minutes later a big burly young man appeared in the shadows of the building. As he got closer, there was no fear in my heart, no pain in my hand and no hesitation that I was not going to let anyone punk me or Marcos. His brother came closer and I could see the younger brother behind him telling him, "That's him, he's the one." When his brother got close enough to where he could see my face. He paused, looked at his brother, took a deep breath and said,

"This is who hit you?" His brother responded with a confident, emphasized, strong,

"Yeah." There was a long silence and the older brother looked at him and said in a soft, wavering voice,

"There is nothing I can do. He beat me up last week, I'm not messing with him."

I busted up laughing. I stepped away and walked towards Marcos's house. As I got to the end of the building I could see Marcos peeking around the corner. He appeared and asked me what happened. I explained and he laughed as hard as I did. This solidified our relationship even more. Marcos knew that as long as he had me around no one would bother him. We continued our walk to his house. When we arrived, we ate ham and cheese sandwiches and drank the real Kool-Aid (made with the flavor, sugar and water instead of just the flavor and water.) I never wanted Marcos to think I was taking advantage of him, or his family's generosity, so I never overstayed my welcome, or came by more than one or two times a week. But on the days where I stood at the gas station to make my few dollars to eat, I thought about Marcos, his family and how lucky he was, yearning for the day when my family would be the same way.

Chapter Six

6

I stood in the middle of a grassy area, ran as fast as I could...

After a few weeks of living in the apartment, things seemed good. I had a new best friend in Marco, an actual bedroom (shared with Travie), three good meals (two at school and the one I got after work) and my attendance at school was good (though my grades were poor). I guess the problem was that though things seemed good I would soon discover they weren't. One Saturday, after a long day at the gas station, I decided to go home instead of eating, I felt like spending time with Travie and Mama, really the whole family, but I knew Bernard and Peanut were not going to be there. For some reason I felt joy, excitement, and happiness. As I skipped towards the apartment, I felt as though we had taken a turn on the road of happiness and I was in the passenger seat enjoying the ride.

As I ran up the stairs there was a strange smell that filled the hallway, like something was burning, but not like the fire in the garage burning, something strange. I didn't really care because I was home, about to enjoy the evening with Mama and Travie. Maybe we could play cards or watch TV. I busted through the door and discovered my worst nightmare had come true. There was Mama sitting on the coach with a crack pipe getting high. My heart dropped and tears rolled down my face. Mama was so high she didn't even know I had come in. I would have never imagined that Mama was capable of doing something like that to herself... to us. She may not have been the most responsible parent, but I knew she would never do anything to jeopardize the lives of her children, or so I thought. This was just icing on the cake, Mama really did not care about us or what happened to us. I could not believe that on top of us not having food in the house or clean clothes on our backs, my brothers and I were going to have to deal with Mama doing drugs. The little respect I had for her was gone and I refused to even look her in her face. I now despised the women I called my mother and I did not care if she was dead or alive. I ran to my room and slammed the door.

As a young kid I knew there were drugs in my community and I had even seen drug deals, dealers, and users. Now my Mama fit into that category. As I sunk deeper into my own world I knew I had to keep myself occupied. The next Saturday was a beautiful day. The sun was high in the sky. There were no clouds in the sky, it was not too hot and there was a slight wind. I went to the gas station early to get a jump on the people who had to fill up for road trips or a day in country, or whatever "normal" people did on Saturdays. My first client of the day pulled up in a sleek black, Mercedes coupe. Wow, what a car. He had a beautiful woman in the passenger seat and the top was down.

I came out from the side of the pillar, my normal hiding spot so the attendant would not see me, and kindly asked him if I could pump his gas for a tip. He looked at me, smiled and said, "Sure kid, fill'r up." Today was gonna be a good day. After I finished pumping his gas the man went to pay the attendant and came back with what I could see as a bill in his hand. I knew I was about to get a whole dollar tip, a large part of my daily earnings on the first pump of the day. I could not show my excitement nor could I let him know I saw the bill. I stood behind the pillar and waited. He came around the corner and handed me a crisp, new ten dollar bill. I could not contain myself.

"Thank you!" I yelled. I was in shock.

"Any time," he responded as he started his car, snapped his seat belt and before I could respond there was a screech of his wheels, some smoke and he was gone.

With this jackpot I was done working for the day and decided to splurge. It was too early for lunch, so I went to the toy shop which was down the street next to the hardware store. I did not know what I was going to buy, but it was going to be special and only for me. I entered the toy store and walked up and down the aisles looking for my special present. Legos? No. G.I. Joe? Nope. Transformers, Optimus Prime... Maybe. Then I saw it... probably not what most kids growing up in South Central, L.A. would yearn to buy, but I knew I had to have it... A kite. It was your basic kite, but I liked it. The picture showed it as red and yellow with a long tail. It was eight dollars, but I didn't care. I took it up to the counter and the clerk asked me if I needed to buy string, because it was not included. I told him it didn't need it 'cause I had some... a lie, but I had a plan. The total was $8.40. I gave him my ten, stuffed the change in my pocket and walked next door to the hardware store to steal my string.

After stealing a spool of string, I made my way to the park down the street. I had never flown a kite, but today was my day to learn. I could not read very well and who had time for directions. I opened the kite and looked at the picture. Not really knowing how to put it together, I guessed and when I was done, it looked good to me. I attached the string and now it was time to launch. I stood in the middle of a grassy area, ran as fast as I could with the kite in my left hand and threw it. The wind immediately picked it up and I held on as tight as I could to the string. The kite soared, higher and higher. The string was coming out of my pocket so fast it felt like it was burning my thigh. I watched the kite and longed to be sitting on its wings like an angel. Before I knew it I had run out of string. I tied the string to my shoe lace and sat down. It was the most peaceful moment I had ever experienced. I watched the kite and felt as though I had escaped to a wonderland, full of my every dream come true. I sat there watching the kite for hours, forgetting about Mama on crack, Junior, my troubles and my life as it existed.

CRACK

Move over equality, I was sent to destroy the black nation.

Bye bye education, they die for me now

They kill, steal, rob, and deal all because of me

At one point their intimate desire was to be free.

My boss's plan worked out to a tee

There were too many running free, so they sent me.

I'm a destroyer, yes, a destroyer of life.

I can make you sell your clothes, your kids, and yes,

even your wife

Try and kill me; in time I'll be back

Stronger, deadlier and indeed hunting for blacks.

You ask who I am indeed, I'm not ashamed

I was sent to destroy the black nation,

hello I'm Mr. Crack Cocaine.

Chapter Seven

I'm special and I deserve a special class.

I never let Mama know that I had seen her that day getting high, but it never left my mind. During the time I was at home I noticed a few things had changed. Mama was distant, Junior was making frequent stops by to "see Mama" and the apartment was seemingly a revolving door for the neighborhood locals. We had people coming in and out of the house at all times of the day and night. Junior was always honest with us about his drug use, so I knew when he was over they were using together. This made things go from bad to worse and to top it off, Mama had a new boyfriend who was a drug dealer. So in my mind Mama was not only using, but selling. I guessed this was why all the people were using our house like the twenty four hour 7-11.

I was mad. I know they say humans don't get mad, they get angry, but I was mad. At school the teachers could not tell me anything. From my stand point, how could they? My Mama could not tell me anything, so how could someone who did not have my blood tell me anything. It was my way or no way. My teachers would kick me out. I would curse them out. I would go to the Principal's office and spend hours there, listening to the women say things about me like I was slow, dumb and crazy. They were the crazy ones. I was my own person and made my own rules. One day someone would get my point. This pattern continued until one day the Principal came out and told me I was going to a new "special" class. That's right. Now he gets it. I'm special and I deserve a special class.

He told me to go to Room 207, which was behind the library. I thought this was great for the most part, a new teacher, new class, new start, but no Marco. I got to the door and saw some of the kids from around the neighborhood who I did not know went to school. I opened the door and in a loud boisterous manner stated,
"I'm here." The teacher rolled her eye and instructed me to sit down and shut up. That set me off. Before I knew it my anger exploded. I cursed her out from front to back and threw a chair at her. The aide mumbled some swear words about my, "crazy ass" and told me to, "get the hell out and go back to the Principal." I obliged by sweeping her papers from her desk and knocking some books off the shelf before exiting. How was this a special class? The teacher was rude and the aide was worse.

When I arrived back at the Principal's office, he already knew about the situation and told me my Mama was on her way up to the school. I responded by telling him,
"I don't give two rats asses about my Mama or her coming to the school." I had always made fun of crack heads in school and now not only was my mother a crack head, she was a crack head coming up to my school. Though I said I did not care,

I really did. I did not want anyone to see her because they would know she was a crack addict. I was embarrassed and knew that it would soon circulate around the neighborhood. Mama never showed up. Good. I sat in the office for the rest of the day and the Principal told me that I could not come back to school for a week. Fine with me... more money, more money, more money.

The next morning I awoke to Junior talking to Bernard about Mama's bizarre behavior. He spoke of her actions when she gets high and how she is not normal. Junior, despite being immature, has always been honest with Bernard and Peanut about Mama's life. So I supposed the conversation I overheard was normal for the two of them. As I stood by the opening to the living room Junior continued to talk. He said last night had come to a head when they were at the apartment. He said that Mama had fallin' to the floor in convulsions. He said she was shaking and coughing up blood which was thick like syrup. Tears filled my eye wells. Was Mama dead? I wanted to go to her room to see if she was there, but I just listened. Junior said he tried to hold down her tongue so she would not swallow it. He said she seized for five minutes and then laid there delirious with a fixed look on her face. He said she did not move, but he took her into the bedroom. He suggested to Bernard that we leave her alone today to let her rest. I heard Bernard ask why, and Junior said,

"She had a rock of cocaine in her mouth the size of a marble and was choking on it during the seizure. That's why she was coughing up blood." I slowly went to Mama's room and opened the door to peek in. Mama laid there silent as if she was dead, but her chest rose up and down, indicating to me she was breathing. I slowly closed the door and went back to my room to get ready for work. Though I wanted to care, I couldn't. All I could think of was making my money and taking care of me.

Later that night after work, I returned home to Mama in the kitchen cooking something, Travie playing and Bernard watching TV. I guess the rule was no one was to say anything about what happened to Mama the day before and eventually it will go away. People knocked on the door for what seemed like every ten minutes until I went to bed. There was nothing my brothers and I could do about the traffic flow in our house, so we just pretended it did not exist. From what I heard Peanut say, the whole neighborhood knew they could get their next fix at our apartment. If that was true it explained the constant stream of hypes in and out, in and out.

The next morning, I awoke to a bang on the door. Was it starting already? It was Sunday, too early for the traffic to begin. I tried to ignore it, but it was steady bang. Everyone else was sleep. I went to the door to see who was so obnoxious to bang on the door that early on a Sunday. I cracked the door with the chain on, just enough to see who it was. To my surprise it was a police officer pointing a .45-caliber pistol at me. I heard him say in a deep voice,
"Open the door, son." I yelled,
"Mamaaaaaaaa."
"Open the damn door, boy." I continued to scream for Mama but she apparently did not hear me. He stated in a very clear voice,
"If you do not open the door, I will shoot you." This scared me and I knew he was serious. I was petrified to know that my life was in the hands of a police officer who was pointing a .45 at my head. I agreed and told him I had to close the door in order to take the chain off.

As I closed the door, I knew there was no way he could shoot me because he could not see me. I ran as fast as I could towards Mama's room, yelling for her at the top of my lungs. I heard a

loud bash as the police busted the door down. I arrived at Mama's room to try and tell her what was happening, but I was too frantic to get it out. Mama was awake and lying in the bed. By the time I had composed myself to tell her, she had already figured it out. I stood frozen like a statue as I heard the police behind me yelling,
"Get to the ground with your hands above your head."
Were they talking to me or Mama?
"GET ON THE GROUND, NOW!" They must have been talking to me. I slowly lowered my stiff body to the floor, as tears rolled down my face. Mama was ordered to the ground as I could hear other police officers yelling at Travie, Peanut and Bernard. As we each were handcuffed, I felt scared, a different scared then I felt in the fire. I knew I was not going to die, but was Mama going to jail? Where would we stay? How could she do this? Didn't she care about our wellbeing?

Soon we were all hand-cuffed and marched out onto the front lawn of the apartment building like the circus main event. Mama was taken to wait in a police car to answer questions with the police sergeant. It was cold. We shivered in the wet mist which covered the grass as we waited for the police to make their decision about what was going to happen next. I could hear the officers tearing through our apartment as glass broke and things fell. I looked up to see the neighbors peeking out of their windows and appear from around corners. As the police made more of a scene, more people emerged just to see who the police were arresting this time. This scene was perfect for the after church gossip for most of these folks. I tried to keep my head down, as I did not want anyone to know it was me or my family. Bernard and Peanut did the same as Travie just whaled for Mama like a little baby. I was humiliated and ashamed.

We now had to face the fact that all our friends and neighbors knew that Mama was selling, and as they probably assumed using. The police came out with the drugs that Mama had on the kitchen table just the night before and carted her away to jail. The neighbors soon dispersed shaking their heads probably in disappointment that they did not get a bigger show. The police told us we were going to stay with Grandma. The day could get no worse... Back to living with Junior. They let us pack some things and took us to her. The rest of the day was spent listening to Grandma talk about how stupid Mama was and that she deserved to go to jail. My life was horrible and I just longed for my kite soaring like an angel, my dreams and inner peace.

Chapter Eight

8

...out of class I never let anyone punk me.

As my home life continued to spiral out of control, my school behavior followed the same pattern. After Mama's arrest and our return back to Grandma's, I did not let the school know what had happened. I went back to the "special class" and tried my hardest to maintain composure. But it never worked. I was too mad. Though school was an escape for me I was not learning because I was always getting into fights, calling teachers names, and throwing things. I made a decision that I had to do better, or I was going to end up like everyone else in the 'hood: hussling, stealing, and using the white man as an excuse for why we would never succeed.

As I turned my academics around, my behaviors slowly improved. School started becoming my avenue to escape my reality and move towards what I wanted later in life.

After the first quarter of being in the special class I made honor roll. I had Marcos to thank for this; he helped me see how school was not that bad if I just listened to the teacher and asked when I did not understand something. My behaviors were better in the class, but out of class I never let anyone punk me. I was hard and I would do what I had to do to prove it. Marcos mirrored what I did out of the class and I encouraged him to stay away from me unless we were at his house. As a good friend, I tried to show him he had it good and not to walk down my path because he had parents and a family who supported him.

One day after a long day of school and work, I arrived at Grandma's to find Mama was there. She had bonded out and was awaiting trial. I was not too happy to see her, as I had gotten used to life without her. Living with my grandmother was much better than living with Mama. We were blessed with a little more food in the refrigerator and did not have to deal with crack addicts coming in and out of the house day and night. We had, until that moment, escaped our Mother and her addiction.

I could see in her eyes that she was upset at me for not being excited. She looked at me and said,
"Ain't you happy to see me, Tay?" I replied with a cold,
"Nope." She replied with rage in her voice,
"I should have let them take your ungrateful ass to jail with me." That was it; I had had it with her and her ways. I looked at her and said,
"You will regret you said those horrible things when I'm dead."

Later that night I went to the backyard where they were almost done with rebuilding the garage. This scene was where I was supposed to die a few months earlier and the neighbors saved me, but no one was going to save me this time. It was time for me to go. I was tired. Tired of life, tired of Mama, tired of Junior, tired of the drugs around me, tired of having to work for myself, tired of the school saying I was bad, tired of being tired. I climbed up to the top of the garage with a ladder they had left for assembling the roof. Whatever small bit of pain I would feel from my fall I knew would be short, because I would die and be an angel in heaven. As I stood on top of the roof all I could think was thank goodness this is it, I will meet my maker and escape this life of hell. I took a deep breath and jumped.

    I hit the ground hard, doing a dirt belly flop a few feet away from the side of the building. I knew I was dead, a goner. But as I laid there waiting to see the proverbial white light, hear the angels sing and the harps play. I realized... I'm not dead, I'm hurt. I was so pissed. Not because of the pain, but because I did not die. How did I not die? What did I do wrong? As I lay there the intense pain set in. My ribs, head, knees and shoulders were throbbing. The biggest pain I felt was in my heart. Why was I not released from this pain? All I wanted was to go to heaven and be an angel to watch over Grandma and Bernard. As I slowly moved to a sitting position, I could hear Mama, Junior, Bernard and Peanut coming out from the building laughing. How could my attempted suicide be funny? Mama approached me and said, "What the hell were you doing?" I told her I was trying to kill myself which made her laugh even harder,

    "Why," she asked. I explained that I would rather die than live life with her. She continued to laugh, brushed my comment off and walked away. How could a mother not be hurt by the fact that one of her children would rather die than be with her? From that day forward I knew I would never shed another tear for Mama, nor feel bad when anything terrible happened to her because as far as I was concerned, Grandma was right, she deserved everything that she got and everything that would be coming to her.

    A few months later Mama was sentenced to a year in prison. This meant that we were going to have to stay with Grandma.

Chapter Nine

9

I knew I had not told a joke, but to them it was stupid and hilarious.

Around the same time Peanut got arrested for stealing a car and was placed in juvenile hall. My family was getting smaller and smaller by the day. Though I knew in the back of my head, I was going to miss Peanut, I thought it was better for him to be there then living with us. At least in juve' he had some protection, three regular meals and I knew at the end of the day he was not going to be the next victim of South Central.

Now that Mama was not around, Junior became even more controlling. He flexed his "muscles" every chance he had to make sure we understood he was the boss. My uncle was an extremist when it came to everything. This was evident in his punishments of me. Travie was too young to get hard whoopings and Bernard was too big, so I was the one who got the majority of his anger. It seemed like almost daily he would push me to the ground, punch me, swear at me or hit me for small mistakes that every child makes. His excessive punishment of me was annoying, but I had to convince myself that one day he would get what was coming to him.

December was here... Winter break had arrived which meant a whole two weeks of working, though I was out on suspension the week before. Christmas Eve was especially great. I made $23 working. I knew that people were in the Christmas spirit while out and about, so they were tipping better than normal. I ran to the toy store, to see what "Santa" would be able to put under the tree for me. Though I knew Santa never visited the 'hood, I could at least dream of a present under our "tree". It really was not a tree because Grandma did not have any money to buy one, so she went in the back, picked a switch off a tree (one she knew was too weak to beat us with) and stick it in a pot with a plant. She would then decorate it with whatever we had around the house: newspaper ads, colorful socks, old oven mitts, anything; and this was our Christmas tree.

A beautiful kite would have been nice, but it would have been too big and I could not risk Junior breaking it. After searching I found the last Transformer Optimus Prime action figure they had which was misplaced tucked in the back of a shelf near the Legos. I looked at it in excitement hoping that Santa, where ever he was, would read my mind and send an elf over to get it for me. After admiring the box for a few minutes I decided that Santa was too busy for me and to ensure I had a present under the tree, I was going to buy it for myself. I brought Optimus Prime along with a small roll of Christmas paper, tape and a red bow. Before going home, I stopped at the quickie mart where I could sit and wrap my present.

I took Optimus Prime out the bag, carefully wrapped him with the beautiful red and green paper, and topped the present off with the big red bow. Though I knew what was inside, I was energized to know that I had a present and it would be waiting for me Christmas morning under the tree. When I arrived home I found that they had let Peanut out for the holidays. It was good to have the family back together. When they saw me with a present they asked where I had gotten it from. I explained that I had bought it for myself and wrapped it so I had something to open on Christmas day. They laughed like I was telling the world's funniest joke. I knew I had not told a joke, but to them it was stupid and hilarious. I was not laughing. They were just jealous that they had not thought of such an ingenious idea and instead of praising me they ridiculed me.

The next morning I woke up, ran to the tree grabbed my present and tore the paper off, as if I had never had a present before in my life. I awed in the reveal of my Optimus Prime. He was perfect. I split the box open, took him out and played with him until the sun set. I might have looked crazy to everyone else, but I had gotten a present for Christmas. The joy of having a present let me know two things: things were going to get better and when I had more control, my life was not going to be like this anymore.

THE GHETTO CRY

Deep in the heart of the ghetto

We search for peace and tranquility, somewhere that is mellow.

This desire lurks deep within our subconscious

Yet unfortunately we know that nobody wants us.

We are the leftovers, discarded as waste

That's why they gathered us up and put us in the cruel, cruel, place.

It's hard to find us in this dense fog, but yet we still exist

We are here in the pitch black dark and in the early morning mist.

If you chop through the fortress, you'll find us deep in the woods.

You might get some bumps and scratches on the way, but you'll find our neighborhood

It's the little poverty bubble secluded from everything else

A land with limited means, that's locked away from all the wealth.

Now when you find us, I hope the pollution in the air don't kill you too

Because the majority of my kind is dying in the dew.

Hopefully when you reach our destination

You'll look for solutions to end our black rain.

Our cry goes on.

Chapter Ten

10

I was nervous when the county department came to take us away.

As spring came, Mama came back to live with us and the same pattern started. She was out all night, slept all day and as long as we did not bother her, she did not bother us. We moved into the apartment upstairs from Grandma so she did not know what was going on and Mama could stay high without hearing Grandma's mouth. My birthday came, was just another day. The only difference was that I could see that I was getting bigger and Mama was having a harder time disciplining me. I was still getting into a mess of trouble in school and suspensions were a dime a dozen in my book. I was often a burden on the family which increased my punishment at home. Whippings from Mama occurred daily, but they soon stopped affecting me. I wanted to show her that she could not do anything to hurt me and that the only one who could hurt me was me.

There were times after whippings that out of frustration, I would claw the skin off my face to hurt myself. To teach me a lesson, Mama would then whip me again, and the cycle would continue with me clawing my face when she finished. I knew she felt gratification from beating me, so I would prove to her that I could do far worse to myself then she could. After a while she would tease me about my reaction to her whippings and she encouraged my brothers to do the same. She thought that reverse psychology would make me stop. It did not work. It would just frustrate me and make me hurt myself more. I understood pain and until someone was willing to listen to me I was not going to stop. So my behaviors in school continued and the beatings at home got worse.

It wasn't until the end of the school year that I learned that Room 207 was special education. They said I had a behavior disorder, whatever that meant, but I didn't care. I had my food, job and as long as every one left me alone, I was cool. I still had perfect attendance (outside of my suspensions) and I got to talk to the social worker about things I did not like. There were not that many kids in my class and we had two teachers. Ms. Jackson, the teacher, was a beautiful woman who I believed really did care about me. She used to encourage me not to give up and often told me that I was going to become something one day. In my rage, she always found time to comfort me and she took the time to help me work through my anger.

One day after throwing a chair across the room, Ms. Jackson took me aside to have one of our heart to heart conversations. As I broke down in frustration and started to cry, I could not hold back. Tears were pouring down my face and I had to tell her. I told her how Mama sold drugs, that the police had raided the house, that Peanut was in and out of juve', that I worked at the gas station for food, that Junior beat us… everything. Ms. Jackson was speechless. I could see her eyes well up with tears, but she held back from letting them fall. She took a deep breath, looked me in my eyes and said she would help me. I knew she would. It would only be a few more days and I could go live with Ms. Jackson. My prayers had been answered. I knew Ms. Jackson cared, but to take me in, that was going above and beyond.

A few days later I was called to the counselor's office. This must be it, the moment where Ms. Jackson would tell me how we were going to get me to her house, my belongings transferred, and how my life in the ghetto was finally over. Though nervous at how the news was going to be broken to Travie, Bernard, Peanut, Mama, Grandma and the others, I did not care. Maybe Ms. Jackson would take my brothers too. As I entered the counselor's office a man looked at me and greeted me with a smile. He seemed nice enough. As I sat in the chair I noticed pictures of his family on his desk. That was going to be me, on Ms. Jackson's desk soon. He started asking me questions about me and my family. I wondered why he wanted to know all this information, but then I guess that's what they had to do when someone was going to adopt a child. Eventually the questions become more like a spelling bee: question after question, drill, drill, drill.

"Does your Mom sell drugs? Does she date someone who sells drugs? Do strange people come to your house and act weird? Does your Mom do drugs? Does your Uncle beat on you? Do you have food in your house..." Where did this come from? Who cares about the past, isn't he supposed to be asking my feelings about living with Ms. Jackson? Then the question that I was waiting for came,

"Do you want to move out of your house and relocated to another place where there are no drugs?" There was no hesitation...

"Of course I want to live with Ms. Jackson!" I yelled out.

The man stopped and paused. He then chuckled to himself.

What was so funny? I did not tell a joke. Why was he laughing? The silence in the office was strange. He then said,
"Son you are not going to live with Ms. Jackson, I am going to make sure you are safe." I was upset, but I did not want him to know. I held back the tears and asked,
"Could we stay at grandmothers so that my brothers and I are not separated?" He agreed that he would try and work that out with the agency. He then told me that he would be going to tell higher authorities what was happening at my home. The next day they came and took the four of us from Mama.

I was nervous when the county department came to take us away. They took me out of school, drove me to Mama's apartment and told Mama,
"You are unfit and losing custody of your children." Boy were Mama, Grandma and Junior mad at me for telling what was going on in our home. Mama started yelling at me calling me stupid and told me that I ruined our family. I can still hear her telling me that she hated me and that she never wanted to talk to me ever again. Once again I regretted telling anyone anything. I felt terrible. All I wanted was to go and live with Ms. Jackson. I felt worthless. As we moved downstairs to Grandma's, I knew this was going to be a problem. Now we were going to be Grandma's burden- her full responsibility and she was going to have to deal with Mama's drug habit. Because Grandma had custody of us, Mama was going to be hanging around the apartment all the time.

Grandma was right. Because Mama did not have custody of us anymore she lost her governmental support and soon after the apartment. Grandma refused to let Mama live with her because she knew what would happen – stealing, more drugs, crazed boyfriends, and total destruction of what she had worked hard to build. Because of Grandma's decision, there would be weeks that we did not see Mama. God only knew where she was and what she was doing. All we knew was that she was probably living on the streets doing what she had to do to survive. She did not want to be around and frankly after what she had said to me, I did not want her to be around.

Chapter Eleven

11

*As I stood there frozen,
I knew that it was my time*

Every time Mama did come around she ignored me and refused to talk to me. I made sure that I did not let what she did affect me emotionally because I knew that deep down inside, what was happening was not right and I had to speak up. There were some benefits to telling the school counselor about what was happening at home. At the start of the next school year he took us to Goodwill where we received clothes. This was great because we did not have to share clothes anymore, especially because we did not have that much following the fire. The trips to Goodwill made me feel like someone did care about us and our well being.

Mama would come to Grandma's house and make trouble by trying to force her way in to steal something to feed her drug habit. Because of this, Grandma's health started to take a toll on her, the trials and tribulations of Mama's drug use wore Grandma down. Mama would harass her about her welfare checks and regularly demanded that she get her "fair share." Mama would repeatedly insist that she should be allowed to move in. Grandma never gave in until one day we saw Mama on the street looking like she was prostituting herself for drugs. Grandma let her return, but she continued to roam the streets, though she said she had cleaned up her act. She even tried to convince us that she had distanced herself from her crack head friends and dealers.

This facade did not stay for long. After a few weeks Mama was back to stealing things from Grandma to buy drugs. Eventually Grandma's money, jewelry and diamond bracelet came up missing. Mama was stripping Grandma of everything she owned and then would deny committing the crimes. Mama started avoiding us again and acted ashamed when we were around and she was high. As much as she tried to hide it, we knew. We could see it in her eyes. She was zoned out for minutes at a time and her body language always gave it up. Grandma was stuck in a difficult situation and often threatened to give us up to a foster home if she did not stop stealing from her. Her response to Grandmas was,

"Give the little bastards away and I'll never speak to you again." Underneath this response I could see the hurt, anger and fear in her eyes. Soon she stopped coming around.

The roller coaster of a life I had seemingly continued as Junior moved in with his wife and daughter, Winter, a few weeks later. All I could think was here we go again. I was bigger now, so Junior was not going to do to me what he had done in years past. Now that Junior was back, Grandma was in more of a financial hard place. To help, my brothers and I stole what was on the shopping list from the grocery store. We each had an item and agreed that if anyone got caught we would run and drop the merchandise we stole. Though we were trying to help, the toll of

Mama's addiction, Junior and his family, and being responsible for us, Grandma had little patience for us, especially me and my antics at school. She began to take her anger out on us because Mama was not around to discipline our negative behaviors. I started avoiding coming home until after nightfall because I knew by then Grandma would probably be too tired to fight or if she did it would be short and to the point. My plan was fine until one night...

One night after a long day of school and working at the gas station, I knew it was time for me to go home. I figured Grandma did not have anything to fuss at me about and the day overall was a good one. After picking up something to eat at my usual spot, I headed down my normal route home. As I approached 28th street, I decided to go to 27th to avoid the light that was about to turn green. This way was, as I called it, the scenic route because there was a large Catholic Church on 27th that had a huge stained glass window lit up at night.

As I turned the corner by the church there was a hidden doorway connected to a small gangway. It was dark and not really noticeable to anyone who did not frequently know the area or paid attention. As I walked past the doorway I felt a large hand grab my arm and yank me into the darkness. As I looked up, a hefty lady pulled my hair and snatched my head back, sticking a sharp object into the side of my neck. Fear came through every ounce of my body, I wanted to go limp and try to escape, but the women said,

"If you say one word or try to move I will stick this screwdriver through your neck and leave you here to die a bloody death." There was strong emotion behind her voice and I knew she was serious.

I tried to escape, but the metal screwdriver was cold as it was pushed closer to cutting my throat. I tried again. Deep inside I did not think she would actually kill me, but then she whispered,

"If you pull away one more time, you'll lay here dead and nobody will know what happened, except for the rats who will watch me kill you." So I stopped pulling, believing that she would kill me. As I stood there frozen, I knew that it was my time. The fire was a foreshadow to the fact that I was never going to be a teenager and that my pointless life would end here in a dark alley by the hands of a crazed lady with a cold screwdriver. I could accept this fate, but inside I wanted to know why was this the way I was going to die.

"Get on your knees," she said softly. I hesitated for a moment and the screwdriver got tighter on my throat. Anything tighter would leave a mark.

"Put your hand down my skirt." I was scared. Petrified. I could smell a horrible stench coming from her. She wanted my hand to go there? Why? I was going to smell like that. Did I have to? I would rather her kill me. My arms were not long enough to reach down her skirt but she insisted I touch it. I hesitated, but moved towards her skirt, I could feel the screwdriver loosen from my neck. She put my hand where she thought it should be and told me to rub. As I rubbed her she would relax, but when she felt like I was not touching her where she wanted to be touched, she would tighten the screwdriver back towards my throat. I whispered,

"Please stop." She kept making me touch her, as tears rolled down my cheeks. No one walked by. No one could see us. This had to be a nightmare and it was time for me to wake up. She slowly slid down the wall and soon sat in front of me with her legs open and the screwdriver to my chin.

"Put your mouth there." I looked and said,
"WHAT?"

"You heard what I said; you know what the hell I am talking about. Put your mouth down there now!" I had no idea what she

was talking about nor did I want to find out. What was I supposed to do? Where was my mouth supposed to go? Why? I started crying harder,
"Shut the hell up and put your mouth down there and do what you know I'm telling you to do, now, and you better not say one more word." I wanted to scream, but I knew she was serious and I was going to have a screwdriver in my neck. She kept whispering that I was taking too long and that she was going to kill me. I could hear footsteps. I paused and hoped they were going to see me and help get me away form her. They continued to walk. As she took her other hand and pushed my head down towards the separation in her legs, the smell became more intense and I could not stand it anymore. I hopped up and hit my head against the brick wall behind me. As she tried to stand up I could see her trying to push the screwdriver towards me. I kicked her in her shin causing her to buckle; I sprinted down the street and around the corner.

When I got home, it was silent; it was like God telling me to be at peace with it. Grandma was nowhere to be found, nor were Travie, Bernard, Junior, his wife or Winter. I went to the washroom and washed my hands. No matter how many times I tried to wash it away, I felt like the smell would not leave. I laid down and closed my eyes. All I could hear was her raspy voice and the darkness of the room reminded me of the alley. I stayed awake hoping that I would fall asleep forgetting what just happened or even hoping that I would wake up from this horrible dream. I never awoke. The next day came and the reality of what happened set in. I had been sexually assaulted, groped and molested and there was no one to tell and nothing I could do about it.

Chapter Twelve

12

I could feel my anger rise.
As my blood started to boil...

After the incident by the church I became very withdrawn. Sinking into my own world, I did not want to interact with anyone, nor let them know too much about what was going on in my head. My family situation did not change no matter how I tried to fight it. I could not escape the drugs and hunger which surrounded me. As word got around about the police raid, Goodwill and Mama's drug habit, kids reminded me of how poor I really was. They laughed at my clothes and even taunted my clean Goodwill apparel. As I sunk into depression, no one seemed to notice that my behaviors at school were my desperate pleas for help.

One Saturday morning, I woke up to Mama and Junior arguing.
"Did you smoke my crack?" Mama asked Junior
"What are you talkin' bout?" Junior responded

"I know you smoked it up Junior." She walked to the bathrooms where my uncle had presumably been. "I can smell the crack in the air from when you were in the bathroom."

I can vividly remember the smell of crack. The smell was so dense and thick it would clog my lungs. The distinct odor is one I will never forget. My mother, father, Junior and his wife would all smoke together. These were the few times that I did get to see Benny when I was young. Hours on end the four of them would smoke and smoke and smoke. They would pool their money together to ensure they had enough crack to maintain their smoking habits for the time they were together. Even though I was young I knew that when Benny was over they were locked in the bathroom smoking crack.

They each had a different reaction to the high. The more we were exposed to them getting high the more obvious it was to my brothers and I that they were high more often than not. Benny could not speak when he got high; when he did try his words were slurred together and blended. This scared me. When I looked into his eyes, I could see the pain he was enduring. He could not look me in my eyes and if I tried to talk to him he would talk but in a bashful and ashamed way. He looked as though he was in the twilight zone; he had no clue as to what was going on around him. There were times when I would purposefully ask my father questions just to see what he would say. I knew he did not want to answer me or even be around me, but I wanted him to realize that I was not stupid and that I knew what he was doing. He would always make and attempt to answer, but the usual response was some garbled up sentence that no one understood. Bernard, Travie and I would often giggle at his reaction to the drug because as little kids we did not know any better. It was like a circus side show.

Junior hummed and rocked back and forth when he was high. He looked like a man without a guitar trying to catch a note. He sat and entertained himself until the high was gone. Unlike Benny, he was able to speak but tried to avoid it at all cost because speaking would interrupt his humming and rocking. Ironically when he was high he was very honest with us about his, and everybody else's, drug use. There was even one time when he said,

"I wish this drug was never invented, but there's nothing I can do to get off it. The drug is calling my name and I have to answer it." While Junior hummed, his wife was completely silent when she was high. She would walk around the house sucking her teeth though there was nothing caught in them. She would try and clean everything in sight.

Of the four of them, when high, Mama was the worst. There were days that she was mild mannered, while other days she would go through fits of rage. She would yell, scream, and even lash out at us. This is what happened when she asked Junior about smoking her drugs. She knew he was high on her drugs, but by him lying it made the situation worse. As the confrontation escalated, I could tell they were about to fight. Junior ran out of the house telling her to leave him the hell alone. Mama followed yelling in an angry tirade. As we made it outside we saw Junior muff Mama so hard she fell to the ground. With a blink of an eye he was on top of her punching her repeatedly in the face. She tried to cover her defenseless body but he had her pinned and it was bad.

Bernard, Travie, and I stood there yelling at him to get off her, but he was so high I did not even know if he could hear us. He kept hitting her and every time we tried to get him off her he pushed us away. By this time the neighbors heard the commotion and came out to see the excitement. Mama and I had our fair share of disagreements and though she had said and done some pretty nasty things to me, at that moment I wished that I could have helped her. After a few more hard punches to the face, Junior just stopped. He leisurely got up and gingerly started to walk back to the apartment. As we watched Mama rise to her feet, her face was full of fresh blood and quickly forming bruises. She grabbed a rock and headed towards the balcony where she knew Junior would be before entering the apartment.

The neighbors watched, as if they were seeing the newest headliner for the WWE. It was fun to them. All they needed was a box of popcorn and a Sprite, but to us it was horrible. This was my family and other people were getting pleasure out of this fiasco of Mama fighting with Junior. I could feel my anger rise. As my blood started to boil, Mama had made it to the balcony.

"Junior," she yelled. As he looked up just as Mama hurled the rock from her hand hitting him square in the nose, it immediately busted and he fell to the ground yelling,

"I'm gonna kill you bitch." Blood was everywhere. I turned to see the neighbors laughing and smiling at the event. I immediately responded,

"What the hell are you looking at, this is none of your business." I could not believe that seeing my family hurt was funny to them.

The paramedics soon came to stitch up Junior and Mama's war wounds. It hurt me to see my family fight like that just because of some crack. This made me hate Mama and Junior even more. They were nothing more than two adults which I had to obey when they asked me to do something. To me Junior was no longer my Uncle, but rather a stranger who lived in the house. And Mama was not my mother, just a lady who came and went like the wind. The worst thing about the fight that day was that I knew that it was not over. It was evident that though they were brother and sister, they hated each other to the core and the battle would never end.

Chapter Thirteen

13

...but this trip would change my life forever.

With all the craziness around the house and news spreading of my family's lifestyle, I felt the need to separate myself from the madness. Though I saw what drugs were doing to my home, I was often tempted to sell dope, as my friends had pressured me time and time again to do so. I must admit I was curious to learn what it felt like to hang out with a group of people who were doing the same thing together and Marcos wanted to see what it was like as well. We saw so many of them committing what appeared to be easy crimes and we wanted to give it a try. So I did as Marcos was not ready.

I wanted to try the easy thing first and move up the ladder to bigger crimes. Previously we had taken things for dinner from the grocery store, to me that was not stealing, but survival. This time I was going to steal something that I wanted, not something

I needed. I could feel my heart racing. It was my turn to try the criminal lifestyle. I fought the inner temptations for so long and now I was giving in. I had it all figured out. I was 'gonna get a gold rope chain. As I walked down the street I scoped out my victim. A few blocks away I could see a boy about my age walking with just the chain I had envisioned. As I got closer, my heart was thumping out of control. When I was two steps away, I looked him straight in his eyes and ripped the chain off his neck. He started to cry. I smiled and started running as fast as I could because I did not want anyone to figure out who I was.

As I ran, I thought, that was easy. I felt pleased and happy. The next step in the plan was to go a few blocks down and pawn it for some quick money. As I slowed to a jog, my heartbeat gradually decrease and I felt like I had overcome a major obstacle in my life. I did it once, so I knew I could do it again. As I took a sigh of relief, I did not notice the group of five boys who had surrounded me. One looked at me and simply said,

"You have something that belongs to my cousin and I will be retrieving his belongings." He snatched the chain out of my hand, turned around and walked away. I was crushed. I had waited so long to steal and now that I had, it was taken from me just as quick as I got it. The lesson learned was simple... I was not made for the life of petty crime and decided to stick to pumping gas and flying kites, for a while at least.

৯•৶

Life at home was the same. Junior and Mama continued fighting over crack, Bernard was always gone, Travie being Travie, and Winter and I trying to stay under the radar. Though Winter was young, she was a smart little girl. I quickly found out that being four, you are like a sponge, copying everything everyone else does, mimicking words, and following adults (or those bigger than you) around like a lost puppy. To many in the house this was annoying and they often got frustrated with her, but I didn't mind, it was kinda cool. Besides I felt like she looked up to me.

Winter was a beautiful little girl. She had fair colored skin and big green eyes which made her look like a princess. Her curly hair was always in two pony tails, though never even. It made her look even more precious. Winter did not have many toys nor did anyone pay attention to her. There were times where she would hide and not be found for hours. I never really understood why someone would have a child to neglect and mistreat them. But I guess this was a common thread in my family and she was no exception, though she should have been with those beautiful angle eyes.

I can remember all Winter wanted was attention. When Bernard would come home, she would laugh and laugh at him making faces at her or while he threw a ball her way. She loved Bernard. I would have liked her to interact with me the way she did with him, but I guess there was something about him that made her love him even more. Though Bernard appreciated her love, he was much older and often didn't have time. He was too busy banging and slanging that he could not give her the love and attention she wanted. She tried to get his love and when she didn't I was there to pick up the slack. It was cool having a "little sister" around. We had a great time together playing imaginary games and playing with the ball in the backyard, which is why what happened, hit me so hard...

One afternoon Bernard said he was headed out for the day and would not be back until later that night. This was nothing new in his daily activities, but this trip would change my life forever. As Bernard left there was an eerie silence, almost like the calm before the storm, but yet it was a beautiful day out, sunny with not a cloud in the sky. Bernard ran down the stairs and out into the street to meet a few gang friends. As he hopped onto the sidewalk there was a large crash. Winter had followed Bernard out the apartment in the street and was hit by a speeding car. Her body was dragged 50 feet down the block.

I could hear the screaming, but this was nothing in the hood. I could hear the commotion as witnesses yelled at the driver. I ran to the window and saw Winter's lifeless body on the ground as the man came to a stop, looked out his window, popped open a beer can, and took a chug. He didn't even get out. The family ran to her side, but there was no hope. She died instantly; her petite body could not handle the impact, the weight of the car, or the dragging. I was speechless. This was the first time someone I truly cared about had been taken from me. I did not know how to respond. Was I supposed to cry? Yell? Get angry? Fight? Scream? I did not know what to do; all I could do was stand there. I couldn't cry. I was filled with emotion, but I couldn't let it out. This was my first lesson in the value of life and how quickly it could be taken at the hand of someone else.

Needless to say the rest of my family knew exactly how to react, or so they thought. They were angry, period. Almost immediately; before the police, ambulance, or coroner could arrive; they started to argue. Junior said it was his wife's fault, she said it was Mama's fault, Mama said it was Grandma's fault, Grandma said it was Junior's fault, and you know Junior said it was my fault. I had nothing to say. In my head I kept thinking a beautiful little girl just died and you selfish, shallow assholes could not see past your own world to realize the true magnitude of the situation. Soon the argument changed from whose fault it was to who was going to pay for her funeral. The worst part was that they were so caught up in blame, greed, and money that they did not even mourn for the life of an innocent child.

Because we did not have much money, we ended up going from house-to-house begging for money for "the little girl who died from getting hit by the car." I was more than willing to do this because in my heart Winter deserved a beautiful funeral; she was a beautiful little girl, who was now a beautiful little angel. This was the best thing I could think of to honor her memory. She was sent to us from heaven and now she returned there to watch over those who watched over her. I had to believe that she was going to watch over me, because that was the only hope I had to fight though the sorrow, an emotion I had never experienced.

In the end, we did manage to get enough money to have a funeral which fit Winter. During the funeral, the burial and the repast all I could think of were the good times we had together. It was like a movie on repeat that played in my head over and over again. As everyone sat there, I could not eat. I walked up to Benny and started to cry in his arms. I missed her, I had never missed anyone, but I missed her. A part of me was gone and was never going to return. When we got home the mood was somber. Mama played Diana Ross, "Missing You" which made me cry again and miss her even more. For that one moment in time, we were a family; we grieved together, cried together and eventually mourned together. But, unfortunately, that didn't last long.

Chapter Fourteen

14

Yet another reason to be in my own world.

Grandma never let the accident with Winter go. Her body started to deteriorate even more as the weight of the death of a grandchild ate away at her soul. As time went on Junior, his wife and Mama went back to their life of drugs, Bernard kept banging, Travie was silly all the time and I was alone. The void Winter's death left in my heart was never filled. I longed to hear her laugh and I wanted just one more chance to play with her. As I tried to escape the madness, Marco was slowly changing as well. He was never around and hung out on the block more and more. One day I saw him with a gun and asked him what had happened. He explained that after I took that chain he felt bad because he knew that if I would have had a gun the result would have been different. I asked him why he did not think about the fact that I should have never done what I did, he simply replied,
"That's not the way of life around here." He had a gun, an

attitude and was running the street with his new friends. I did not want any part of it. From that day on I never spent any more time with Marco. Yet another reason to be in my own world.

As months went by, I kept to myself while Mama and Junior juiced Grandma for everything she had: money for bail, cosigning for cars, and her government checks. They continued stealing from her, cursing at her and belittling her existence. They did not realize that Grandma had become so weak from their manipulating ways, sheltering 8 children and four adults in her apartment because they were too busy smoking, dealing, and supporting their habits which were now spiraling out of control. Every evening I would watch her as tears rolled down her face because there was nothing she could do. As time went on I saw the foundation of our family slowly expire as the weight of others and their burdens took a toll on her.

Mama was on speaking terms with Benny, (which really meant smoking terms) and Junior and his wife were the same. Their behaviors made life miserable and though Christmas was right around the corner, I just wanted to forget that it was the holiday season. These were the times that I was supposed to celebrate and rejoice with my loved ones, but I did not have any of that. Last year I bought myself a present, but this year I just wanted to disappear. Grandma did not have the strength to put together a Christmas limb, and I knew neither Mama nor Junior were going to do it. There was going to be no Christmas dinner, songs or gifts under the tree, so to me December 25th could come and go just like all the other days. Unexpectedly, the school ended up taking us to get free toys, giving me at least a few things to play with. That was a nice surprise.

I spent Christmas break pumping gas and coming home to Grandma whose health was deteriorating from arthritis and cancer. She was now bedridden and needed help with every basic function. Her beauty had faded away and she was left with nothing. I was sad, but did not know how to cry. Winter was gone, Grandma was very ill, and Mama and Junior were too selfish to change their addictive ways to help the women who had brought them into this world. I felt like the grey skies that loomed over us were turning darker and there was no hope for sun. I resented Mama and Junior, they continued running the streets, dealing and smoking while Grandma lay in her hospital bed too weak to walk, smelling of urine and fecal matter because no one was there to help her go to the bathroom or change her diapers. I could see the pain in the eyes. I knew she felt abandoned and alone. I wanted to help, but I could not, I did not know how. Grandma was my savior. She showed me she cared when no one else did. She was the only relative I had and now she was helpless left to die at the hands of her ungrateful strung out children.

Soon Grandma's sickness got the best of her. She was immediately moved to the intensive care unit at the local hospital. I did not want to go and see her in that state. The last memory of Grandma at home was looking her in her eyes, which were filled with tears. She could not speak but I knew she wanted to let go, but just couldn't. Two days later as Bernard and I were listening to the latest song from The Boys, "Happy" the phone rang. It was 11:30 PM and I knew it was nothing good. The phone never rang that late. Mama burst into tears, crying uncontrollably and screaming. The energy left my body as she told us Grandma was called to be with God, Winter and the rest of the family. She was gone. I knew this day was coming, but it was not supposed to be then. I looked at Bernard as we both sat at the end of the bed and wept silently. The words of "Happy" continued to play softly as I thought about Grandma being with the Lord, smiling with Winter. With no more pain and admiring her new wings, she was an angel now.

The moment was short live because Mama in full dramatics ran out of the house screaming for Grandma. We had to run after her for fear she might do something crazy. In all the commotion, our church Bible study teacher came out of the house to console her. He stated he knew that this day was coming and he had prepared a verse for Mama to listen to from the Bible. He scoped her up in the middle of the street and comforted her as he recited line and verse from the Bible. He spoke of life after death and being free from pain and sin. Knowing Mama was taken care of, I went back in the house. All I wanted to do was sleep, to block away the pain. I lay there reminiscing about Grandma and her antics: shooting at Junior and his wife, cursing at Mama and creating the Christmas limb. Before I knew it I was sleep.

I could see Grandma in her chair. Rocking. I hugged her and said,

"I knew you weren't dead." She asked me why I would think that because she would never leave me. I put my arms around her and embraced her, never wanting to let her escape my embrace. Unfortunately it was all a dream. When I awoke I was crushed. My heart was full of sorrow. I lay crying into my pillow until day broke. When Bernard awoke I told him what I had dreamt. He was scared, but he mourned again with me. I could not believe she was really gone. What was going to happen to us? Who was going to take care of us? Where were we going to stay? What were we going to eat? Were we going to a foster home?

Grandma left me in the dark the night she passed. I knew my life was only going to get worse from then on. She had been the world to us; she saved us from being split up when Mama lost custody of us. She gave us a better life, even a glimpse of what happiness could look like. Though she was a mean old lady, she gave us her heart. We lived for her "keeping it real" and we knew we could depend on her as our Grandma. I knew now the turmoil was really about to emerge. I could not bear the reality of missing not only Winter, but now Grandma too. I struggled to come to terms with her death and our fate.

Chapter Fifteen

It looked like an imposter was laying there.

A few days later, Mama sent Travie to go live with our cousins in Compton. Mama and Junior did not know how they were going to pay for the funeral and did nothing but argue over the issue. As the argument escalated, the tension in the house got thicker. Mama and Junior were using more heavily and were not focusing on the funeral. Mama rarely came home, as she would rather roam the streets looking for dope to smoke. The hatred that I felt towards Mama grew day by day. The more she did not come home the more I hated her. When she did come home she was high and only said one thing,

"Did the check come yet?" Then the day came where I lost every last bit of respect for her that could have been looming in my mind.

It was late and Bernard and I were in the room with the door closed listening to music. We were the only ones home because Junior was out doing whatever he did with his wife, Mama was gone and our cousins (Junior's other kids) had been taken away by the authorities because of the accident with Winter. We could hear Mama stumble in the door, so we quickly turned the lights off and pretended to be asleep, as we both did not feel like dealing with her. We could hear the door to the room slowly open. Mama was checking on us, but then the door abruptly slammed. We both looked at each other, sat up, and smiled because we had fooled her. Thinking nothing of it we continued listening to our music. About five minutes later we heard moans coming from Grandma's room.

As I glanced at Bernard we both could not believe what we were hearing. Mama was having sex in Grandma's bed. Mama and Junior were so neglectful that they had not thought to see beyond their own worlds to put together arrangements for Grandma. Yet Mama could find some man to have sex with in Grandma's bed before she was even in her final resting place. My stomach turned with disgust. Was I supposed to respect this woman? I could not sleep. How could she be so self humiliating and disrespectful to her mother? When morning came, I went to see if she was home. To my repulsion she was laying in the bed half nude next to the man, they were both sleep. I slammed the door and ran out the house to school not returning until late that night. I knew she would not be home because she was always out walking the streets with her druggie friends.

By the time I got home, Bernard had drowned himself in old pictures of Grandma. He looked depressed. I joined him to comfort him and recall the good times with our angel. A week later the plans for the funeral had finally come together. The selfishness of Junior and Mama had lead to this day not occurring until three weeks after her death. I had only been to one other funeral and this one, more than Winter's, hit me like a ton of bricks. Overall the funeral was beautiful, but Grandma looked like plastic. It looked like an imposter was laying there. Though it did not look like herself, she looked peaceful, like she was in a deep sleep. This brought a tear to my eye, but not of sadness, rather of joy. I remembered the funny things she did and more importantly how tough of a woman she was. This gave me strength. I could rest now. I knew she was resting in heaven. I could finally say goodbye and tell her that I would meet her when I earned my wings.

As we drove to what I thought was the burial ground, Mama told us that we were going to have her cremated. To me this was wrong. If that was the case they should have had it done three weeks prior. Mama then went on to say that they did not have enough money to pay for a burial plot and that cremation was the only solution. It was ironic that they did not have money for a plot but they had all the money they needed for drugs. I was amazed to hear the lies that came out of Mama's mouth. I was stunned that crack had turned Mama into a malicious self centered women who could not even give her mother a proper funeral. As I tried to process this new information, all I could think of was would the ashes go?

Chapter Sixteen

16

We stayed in the brush for at least an hour...

For a while Mama carried the ashes around with her. I guess that was her way of memorializing Grandma. To me it was all a show. Eventually they remained where ever Mama sat them, and then one day they disappeared. I have no idea where they went and I never saw them again. As things got back to "normal" I had made up my mind... The only person who had cared about me was gone and I had nothing to live for. My previous attempts to harm myself were fruitless efforts, so I decided that I was going to live for me. No rules, no consequences and no one could tell me what to do or how to do it.

One night as I walked home from the gas station I noticed Peanut and Bernard outside the house with a bunch of bags piled on his friends car. As I got closer, I saw three bags full of grocery store items. The amount could have fed us for a week.

I was shocked and happy.

"How did you get all this food?" I asked, as I got in shouting distance. They laughed and told me they had robbed a group of people, took all their money and then went to the store and bought everything I saw in the bags. He said that they were going to "feast off their rewards." I did not quite know what that meant, but I smiled and indulged in cheese puffs and soda before going inside.

The next day, as I watched TV, with my new associate (not a friend, just a boy from the neighborhood who was down to do adventurous things), Greg, we looked around the house to find there was nothing to eat, which was shocking cause Peanut and Bernard had just gotten all that food the night before. Though I had my regular dollars from pumping gas, I did not want him to know I had money to spare to feed him. So I turned to Greg and told him that we should rob some people, like Peanut and Bernard did, so we could go to the grocery store and buy food. Greg agreed.

We left Grandma's house and headed towards the local nightclub. We figured that with the type of people who frequented that spot, someone coming out of there was bound to have enough money for us to steal to buy food. As we approached the corner, we spotted a man getting off the bus. My thought was that being Friday, he had just gotten paid, he was headed to the club for some entertainment and that he would be the perfect person to jack. I pointed him out to Greg. As we moved closer, we saw a man standing in front of the club who was watching us. Armed with butcher knives we knew we could take anyone who came close. As the man across the street continued to eye us, we gave him the finger and moved in for the steal.

The man, who had just got off the bus, noticed the situation that was unfolding and started to run. We took off after him yelling,

"Give us your money!" He was too fast, we could not catch him. As we slowed down to catch our breath we both knew that was not how things were supposed to go. I insisted that we try again, so we started walking back towards the club to find another victim. As we walked we noticed the guy we had flipped off heading towards us. When we got closer we saw a group of men behind him. As we saw the number increase, shots rang out.

We turned and ran. As we ran we could hear the bullets ricocheting off cars and iron fences. The sound was clear, as if they were whizzing next to our ears, hitting objects to the left and right of us.

"Ping... ping..." we ducked behind a car. Bullets were flying everywhere. My heart was pounding out my chest. They ran on the other side of the car. They did not see us. We were terrified. As they were looking ahead we ran behind them and into a yard behind an apartment building. This route gave us the advantage because we had gone in full circle around them. We found a bunch of dense bushes to hide in. As they continued to circle around looking for us, we could hear them asking people passing by if they had seen us. We stayed in the brush for at least an hour, ultimately ending up sneaking out and sprinting back to Grandma's place, facing the same hunger we had a few hours before, but now even more terrified that we were "wanted."

Not long after my attempt to rob the man on the bus and getting shot at, did the US Marshal come banging on the door. I was hoping they were not there for Bernard, as Peanut was already locked up, but something told me they were coming for me after the night near the club. As I peaked around the corner to hear the conversation they were having with Bernard, the fact was that they were not there for Bernard or me, but to evict us. Mama and Junior had not paid the rent since Grandma passed and they were there to tell us that we had two days to get out. They instructed us to take our food, clothes and furniture out of the house and that we could not come back. Mama was not surprised as she knew they would eventually come because she and Junior had smoked away every penny.

As soon as the Marshal left, Mama ordered us to start packing and told us she would return later. Mama returned the next morning, higher than any kite I had ever flown. She immediately went to her room and shut the door. As I continued to pack I found a small bit of crack. I knew Mama and Junior did not know it was there because if they had they would have smoked it. Carefully picking it up, I placed it in a baggie and told Bernard I would be back later. Running out the house, I knew exactly where I could go to sell it; the same place we had seen Mama with her friends. I was consumed with the fact that I was about to make some quick, easy cash.

Down the street, around the corner, through the alley and up the block. I soon came across a doped out crack head. It was easy to let him know I had his next fix. He begged me for it. Though he was desperate, he told me he did not have any money, but would make it up to me. In my head I said, "Not today buddy," and kept looking for the cold hard cash. The next lady I came across was a little more coherent; she said she would give me $100 for the crack. I quickly obliged, as she handed me the money and I gave her the small baggie. I could not do anything but smile from ear to ear. I had successfully completed my first drug deal. It was not too hard, nor did I feel any pain. Though I was scared of the repercussions, I knew I had $100, which was a lot of money. The power of crack was a strong thing and a big money maker. I knew I could go home and make more crack, to make more money, but as I walked I remembered that I had to prepare to move.

I stopped at the store and bought a pair of shoes, pants, and a shirt. I then went across the street and bought some food. I felt like the luckiest person in the world to make $100 in ten minutes. I stored the new items in the backyard until I could get them, since I did not want Mama or Bernard to see them. I slipped back into the house and packed with a smile on my face. Soon, Mama woke up and acted like everything was normal. She did not mention moving, nor pack anything. Bernard and I were puzzled about her lackadaisical attitude. Early that evening, Mama finally spilled the news, we were going to live in Compton with our cousin Jeanie. This is where she had sent Travie. I hoped it would not be too bad, but I knew it probably was. Jeanie had seven kids of her own, plus Travie and now the three of us in a four bedroom apartment, nothing good was going to come out of this situation.

I did not know what was going to happen to Junior. His wife was going to jail for child neglect for Winter's death and the death of one of their other children three years earlier. All I could hope was that our other cousins in foster care would be alright and that maybe there they would be able to escape the madness that we had endured. They could hopefully make something of themselves. Beyond that I knew I could not think of them because I had to focus on a different obstacle... Compton.

STRUGGLING

When your entire family lives in the ghetto, from your cousin Tear, to your Aunt May
YOU KNOW YOU'RE STRUGGLING.

When the light bill is in your name, the gas in your brother's, and the bill collectors are after your mother,
YOU KNOW YOU'RE STRUGGLING.

When the cops are on your back cause your mama smoke crack,
YOU KNOW YOU'RE STRUGGLING.

When you're so broke you have to cash food stamps for some soap
YOU KNOW YOU'RE STRUGGLING.

When you have to cash in cans to get some pro-wing style vans,
YOU KNOW YOU'RE STRUGGLING.

When you have to fight to stay off your knees, get up early in the morning to help folks with their groceries,
YOU KNOW YOU'RE STRUGGLING.

When times get too rough and you have to go out and beg cause you don't have enough,
YOU KNOW YOU'RE STRUGGLING.

When your hunger turns to anger and your anger turns to hate, you stop caring and welcome all fate.
YOU KNOW YOU'RE STRUGGLING.

When your ignorance gets the best of you, with survival as your guide, you stop begging and pleading and welcome savage ways to survive
YOU KNOW YOU'RE STRUGGLING.

Chapter Seventeen

...if I wanted to eat, I had to work.

We moved into Jeanie's apartment that evening and almost immediately conflicts arose. I could tell that she was an unstable woman who had many different personalities. She, like Junior, took her frustrations out on kids and used her size to intimidate everyone. She was a big, tall, burly woman which she used to establish control over everyone under her roof. She would beat her kids until they bled and did not want anyone happy, even if she was happy. Being that I had told myself no one was going to tell me what to do, this did not work with me.

As we got settled into the new environment, I noticed that Jeanie did not like to clean, nor take care of herself, her kids or anyone else. Occasionally she would demand that we clean the house, but never did she insist we clean our bodies. Needless to say all of our personal hygiene was awful. Jeanie would use socks as personal hygiene implements and then throw them in the trash for all to see. We showered once a week, if we were lucky twice. Being an active 12 year old, living in hot California, this lack of personal care made me pure funky. All 11 people in the house lived day-to-day without a connected purpose, theoretically ignoring biological and health needs and most importantly we all tried to stay away from Jeanie.

Mama and Jeanie never spoke; they would bad mouth each other, letting the children spread the latest "beef". Bernard and I walked on eggshells as we knew if Jeanie got mad she would threaten us by saying she would kick us out. This fueled my desire to sell more crack. I was not going to be homeless and penniless because of some woman. I felt responsible for my own survival and if I wanted to eat, I had to work. I knew my parents were not going to feed me, Jeanie did not care and Bernard was trying to fend for himself. The kids I met in the neighborhood did not help. They encouraged me to sell crack too. They did it and had nice clothes, jewelry and all the lunch money any one person could handle. Selling crack, though glamorous in my eyes, was not what I wanted to do. Because I saw what it had done to Mama, Benny, Junior, and our family. I just could not do it as enticing as it was.

Instead I continued to pump gas and I got a job at the hamburger stand cleaning up at night, which kept me out of that house. I was paid under the table, which was good because that meant I got cash. No one knew I worked there until they came to eat one day and saw me. My drive for money and personal survival fueled my negative attitude towards my teachers. I did not care about what they said, or what they taught. There was nothing they could tell me that I needed to learn. Because of that, I went to school every day and ended up getting kicked out of class. They stopped suspending me because they knew if they did, I would be out of school all the time. I regularly cursed out the teacher, threw chairs and got into fights. I was unstoppable. Kids were scared of me, adults were scared of me and I did not care. This was my life.

Outside of school and my deviant behaviors, things evened out. I was getting bigger and bigger. People were starting to appear intimidated by my size, which amused me. There were days when I would walk down the street, going to work, and beat up any random person I saw, just because I could. It was funny to me and I could get some anger out on an unknowing soul. I knew no one was going to stop me, so I thought why not. I was regularly recruited by Bernard's gang, but I was too focused on my money to have time for that. I was my own gang.

Exactly one year after Grandma passed away we got the news that my grandfather passed. His death was unexpected because none of us even knew he was sick. I never spent time with him, but that did not mean I did not love him. He and Grandma had been divorced, so most of our time was spent with her. Beyond feeling a little bad that he had died, I did not mourn. I didn't have those feelings. His home was up for sale and going through the foreclosure process, but that did not stop Mama and Junior from their ignorant, greedy ways. They inherited about $16,000 each after everything was settled, which allowed for one thing... all hell to break loose.

Mama gave Jeanie $2000 in rent, which was just enough for two months, gave the three of us $700 to spend, then rented a limo and took her boyfriend out on the town for fun. They were both on drugs and we knew they were going to do one thing... smoke it away. That day Mama drove off in the limo and we did not see her for two weeks. When she did return she had nothing left but the clothes on her back. I could not believe she spent over

$12,000 in under two weeks. What pissed me off even more was that we could have used that money to get our own place again. But instead she looked out for herself, her man of the hour and her habit. Junior did the same thing. I was enraged inside. Jeanie even had the nerve to be angry, not at Mama's actions, but that Mama did not give her more money. Jeanie felt like she was entitled to more and Mama obviously disagreed. This caused for regular arguments, when finally three weeks later Jeanie kicked us out, with no return on the two months' rent.

We were forced to move to the Dalivarden minus Travie who seemed to fit in just fine with Jeanie. It was a motel in poor condition in downtown Long Beach. The water ran brown and there were roaches everywhere. I figured we would not be here long cause Mama had nothing. Bernard was rarely around (he got a job at the local drugstore) and I wasn't giving up anything. I continued to pump gas, but my days were long as now I had to travel an hour and a half to school each way. Being thirteen sucked. Mama would frequently ask both of us if we had any money. Even though we did, we would reply, "nope." As the next few weeks went by Mama started sobering up. There were more positive interactions between the three of us and she was around more. Though we did not have much money I saw she was trying. She even got a job at a hotel down the street, which was nice because just as she established her job there we were kicked out of the Dalivarden. Her job gave us a place to stay with cheaper rent and a nice view. I was beginning to think the sun was starting to peak around the corner of the clouds that has consumed my sky for so long.

Chapter Eighteen

I was trying to clean up my act...

The new place was great. Mama told us the rent was half as much as the last place because she was an employee and we got to see her a lot more. She was at work while she was at home. Bernard and I would often joke that we were "movin' on up" like The Jefferson's because we had a kitchen and the rooms were bigger. Mama was doing better; she was presumably clean, as we had not seen any of her crack friends around, or any of her crack habits. She even started going to church. Bernard was still working at the drugstore and I was trying to clean up my act in school by at least trying to stay in class, though I struggled with others telling me what to do. Travie was still with Jeanie, so it was just the three of us starting to build better relationships. Benny started spending time with us and this made me feel like a real family. Things were really good, until the devil got the best of Mama again.

She once again got hooked on crack, we did not know until one night she stayed out all night, did not report to work and came home the next morning completely high. Though Mama had her setback, Bernard and I continued to progress. I started selling Baseball cards to my teachers for additional money and this proved to be good income. We maintained without Mama who was walking towards the gates of hell and we could not stop her. One night she stole a gold ring right off my finger to get crack. I could not even confront her. I knew it was pointless. I should have known she would stoop to that level since she had stolen from me before. The good thing about our current situation was that because it was just Bernard and I, we got to spend a lot of time together. We wanted to stay away because we never knew when she was going to be at home or if she was going to be high or coherent. We would go to the mall for hours on end. We became each other's support and family. I had not grown this close to anyone since Grandma and Winter had passed, so I was hesitant to get close to Bernard even though he was my big brother. As we bonded I realized he was all I had. So I decided to show him how much he meant to me.

I worked hard as Bernard's birthday approached. I wanted to make it special for him, it was a big day for him… he was turning 16. I knew I could not get him a car or something big, but if anyone was going to acknowledge him, it was going to be me. On his day, Mama was gone, Benny was missing, and he was at work. I gathered all the money I had and counted it to ensure I had enough. I anxiously waited for him to get off work so I could reveal the big surprise. He came home a little after 5:00 PM. I was in my best outfit. I immediately jumped up and told him to change because we had to go. He was perplexed, and though reluctant, changed out of his work shirt. When he was ready I told him that I had a big surprise for his 16th birthday. He laughed and asked what I possibly could give him because I had no money.

I laughed back and told him I found a way to make the day perfect.

We left the house and headed to the bus. After paying for his ride, we arrived at the mall 45 minutes later. He was still a little confused, but seemed interested more than anything. I told him that I was taking him to dinner. He smiled and we entered the Sizzler. I paid for his unlimited salad bar and a steak, and I got just the salad bar because I liked the chicken wings. He was overwhelmed with gratitude and I could see the appreciation on his face. He hugged me, thanking me for remembering and caring enough to do something for him. I knew I had done something really special for him. As we sat and ate until I thought we were going to explode, I knew that I was never going to forget the feeling I had by doing something special for the only person alive I cared about. I knew that day would solidify our bond forever.

A few days later there was a bang on the door. It was the manager, who pushed his way in and told Mama she was fired and had to move out by the end of the month. During the conversation he alluded to the fact that she has stolen some money and bought drugs. I looked at Bernard who told me it would be ok. I looked at Mama in disgust and left to go make some money, which was the only thing I knew how to do. I knew this meant that we were going to have to move, but where? Unfortunately, two weeks later we were back with Satan burning in the depths of hell, better known as Jeanie's.

Nothing had changed. It was still dirty, nasty and Jeanie's attitude was worse than ever. She felt like she had even more power because she knew Mama needed her and her apartment. She would regularly remind us that she was in control by saying,

"Remember whose house you're in." Every chance she got she would use her words to demean us and make us feel weak and powerless. Mama left. I guess she could not stand swallowing her pride every time she came home. She came around once a month to get her check, pay rent and give us $20. Beyond that she was gone to go smoke the rest of her money away. Jeanie would tell us,

"Your mother's worthless. She doesn't really care about you and if she did she would not have you stay here." I had my own opinions about Mama, but I did not have to listen to anyone else talk crazy about her. I hoped that Mama could change again. I knew that if Jeanie gave her an opportunity, she might come around, both physically and emotionally. But until then, I was going to continue to make my money and mind my business.

Chapter Nineteen

19

...I'm gonna kill you, you ungrateful bastard.

One night, after work, Jeanie was in one of her moods. As I walked up the driveway towards the apartment building, she approached me shouting,

"Where the hell have you been?" This immediately sent sparks through me body. Absolutely no one yelled at me. I could feel my blood pressure begin to rise.

"I was working," I aggressively responded. She knew that I was working because she has seen me in the hamburger stand before. Though I had been pumping gas that night, she did not need to know that. With no warrant she responded,

"You're a worthless dumb ass." I knew that I had done nothing wrong or different and if this conversation were to continue any longer it would result in nothing positive as I could feel the heat coming off my face.

"Okay, I'll be that." I responded nonchalantly as to try and end the conversation. But unbeknownst to me that infuriated her even more. I guess she wanted to engage in a battle with me. Today was the day she had picked the "mess with Eboni" card.

"You gotta quit your job. If you go back you will not have a place to live, 'cause this is my house and you will do as I say." I exploded in anger and rage, charging towards her. I had never lost my cool at home like I did at school, but she pushed me to my limit and once there, I was not turning back.

"I don't give a damn what you say. I'm gonna work anyway." As my voice got deeper, I could see the expression in her face change from demanding to petrified. I could see the terror in her eyes; she thought I was going to hit her. By this point everyone had come out the house to see the commotion. Bernard stepped closer to be there if he had to move in and her boyfriend grabbed me, to try to manhandle me away from her. This only increased my anger and strength. I was like a solid mass, unmovable. The rage had taken over. She tried to stand firm, but I could hear her voice tremble,

"Get the hell out of my house and never come back." I spit in her face and walked away to get my things. I packed every ounce of my belongings in a trash bag. Bernard and Travie watched in fear, while my cousins stood on the outskirts of the room gazing at me like I had lost my mind. As I grabbed my bag of clothes and headed for the door, Jeanie came out of the kitchen with a butcher knife, pushed me into the bathroom and held it right to my throat. Screaming,

"I'll kill you, I'm gonna kill you, you ungrateful bastard. I'm gonna kill your black ass for what you just did to me, you're gonna die for rushing me like that." I was angrier than I had ever been. I stared her in her eye and egged her on,

"Go ahead you stupid bitch. Kill me. At least I won't have to live here no more. Kill me, I'd be better off anyway. I don't care if I die. Kill me, bitch." She paused and looked at me as if I was crazy. She had expected me to wilt, but I did not give into her threats. She was stunned.

"Get the hell out my house!" She exclaimed as she pushed me out the washroom towards the door. As I exited out the door and down the stairs, I looked back to see Bernard watching me. I did not want any of them to see me cry, so I put my sunglasses on. As I walked down the street tears poured out from under the glasses and I struggled to keep them from fogging up. I was upset, not at what happened, but at the thought that I was not going to see Bernard for a while.

I had been talking to Peanut on and off, so I figured that maybe I could go live with him. He was in a juvenile halfway house in Canoga Park and I had visited him a few times by bus, which was a four hour ride away. I figured that I could stay there even if it meant a new school and no friends. I headed towards his home, though I knew that I was going to have to listen to different adults, but I did not care as long it was not Jeanie. As I started my journey, it was late and raining. As I made my transfers and the bus rolled on, I kept my glasses affixed to my face so people did not know I was sleeping. The travel took longer than expected because Canoga Park was flooded from heavy rains. When the bus came to my stop I grabbed my bag and proceeded to get off the bus. It had rained so much there was water up to the first step of the bus. I jumped onto the curb and onto the sidewalk, just to get soaked to mid-calf with rain water. It was 3:00 AM when I got to the door of the half-way house. Because it was late I went across the street to Winchell's, a 24 hour donut shop. I sat in a far corner booth, clutched my trash bag and slept with my glasses on.

When morning came, the streets were drying out and I went to the halfway house. I rang the bell and a lady answered. She was the house supervisor. She remembered me. I tried to put on the charm, asking if I could stay there with Peanut. I explained

that I had nowhere else to go. I knew she was going to ask about Mama, but did not know she would ask about Benny. Immediately, to guarantee that I could stay there, I told her I did not know where either of them were, though I knew how to get a hold of Benny if I really wanted to. She then asked the unthinkable...
"Do you want to go to a foster home?" My heart dropped. I wanted to stay there with Peanut.
"Why can't I stay here with my brother?"
"It's against the rules. You have to be placed here by the courts." She then picked up the phone and started to call the authorities. All I could think of was going back to Jeanie's. That scared me fast enough to confess.
"I know where my father is and I have his number." She was confused and wanted to know why I had lied. But in the end she called him.

Benny was livid that I had gone to the juvenile detention center looking for a place to live. He gave the lady directions to his place in Inglewood. She gave me the directions, bus tokens, and sent me on my way. I was nervous because I had no idea what to expect from my father or what it would be like to live with him. All I kept telling myself was that anything was better than living with satan. I did not know much about Benny except that his habit was like Mama's and that I would probably feel like I was living with a male version of her. Had I crawled into a deeper hole than the one I was trying to escape? Should I have gone to foster care like the women at the juvenile center said? At least in the foster home, I would have warm meals and a bed to sleep in, or maybe foster care was just as bad. The fear of the unknown had me so scared to explore my options that, as I rode to Benny's, I debated going back to Jeanie's. The closer I got to Benny's, the more my heart raced. Though I knew Benny did not expect to have one of his son's living with him, I guess he would have felt guilty about turning his back on me.

Benny lived in a motel like we used to live in. After a talk about how things would be, I made myself comfortable in the small space and fell asleep. Living with Benny was not as bad as I thought. He gave me money for lunch and always had food. He even had a job at the local dry cleaner where, from what he said, several of our family members worked. He said the job paid pretty well and he seemed content. Though things on the surface appeared to be smooth, I knew Benny was using. The difference was he was much better than Mama at hiding it.

Benny never was high around me. He had created a balance between his responsibilities (work, bills, food and me) and his drugs. He kept this up for a while, but then, like Mama, the drugs slowly started to consume him. They started to soak up more and more of his money and his time. There were days where I did not see him and when he returned he would act as if nothing had happened. I could tell that my time with Benny was slowly coming to an end. One morning there was a knock on the door and my short, "normal life" with Benny was snuffed out like a candle in the wind.

Chapter Twenty

we were going to be a family and do family things...

The knock revealed my worst nightmare had come true... It was Jeanie. Benny had called her while he was out getting high and told her she had to come and get me because he could not take care of me anymore. I was devastated that Benny would do me like everyone else had. I was saddened by the thought and feeling that he abandoned me. While I collected my clothes all I could think about was that hell hole I was about to return to. As we walked to the car we saw Benny walking down the street. It was obvious that he was high because he did not even acknowledge us. This made Jeanie flaming mad. The ride home was awkward; I did not say one word to her and she returned the favor. Once again I had no control of where I lay my head at night or who I had to put up with to survive. As we pulled into the driveway of the apartment, my heart fell to the ground because I knew what awaited me on the other side of that door.

Everything was just as it was when I left... dirty. Nothing had changed in the months I had been gone. I was extremely overjoyed to see Travie, but even more excited to see Bernard and to my surprise Mama was there. Unfortunately she was more depressed than I had ever seen her. Her state was probably due to her lack of money and resource to obtain her next fix. I would have liked to hope that it was because she was so worried about my well being, but at this point in my life I knew better. Because Mama did not take a stand for me and due to Benny's "negotiations" for her to take me back, I was prohibited from working at the Hamburger stand. So I had to come up with another method to make money.

The next day I went to the discount store and bought a boat load of candy. My thought was to sell it individually and make a profit. I had to learn at what price to sell it for so that I was not over or under charging, but in the end it really did not matter because I knew the kids loved candy and that Jeanie would never know about this hustle. A few weeks into my plan, the school found out that I was selling candy and they threatened to suspend me if I did not stop. I didn't stop. If they asked I would deny it and then there would be nothing they could do. This plan lasted for a while until the kids decided that they did not like my selection of candy anymore. This was just in time too because Jeanie started asking questions.

"Where did you get that money? Are you stealing from me boy?" She asked. It was beyond me how you steal something that was not missing, but I just went on with my day and ignored her. Hearing her nagging and complaining did not last for long. About seven weeks after returning to Jeanie's my prayers were answered. Mama had some friends who owned an apartment building in Long Beach and they offered to help her move into the apartment and live there if she helped clean the premises. We were moving out!!!!

Mama, Bernard and I moved into a one bedroom apartment, while Travie stayed with Jeanie to finish at his elementary school. I guess Mama thought it would be easier to take care of two children rather than three. Peanut was now being taken care of by the courts and the judge determined what happened to him. Every time Peanut got out, he seemed to do something else to go back. I started to think he liked being there rather than with us, but who could blame him?

Our new apartment brought promise for Mama; she said things were going to be different. I thanked God for giving us one more chance and I knew that we were going to make the most of it. Mama said she was going to be clean and stay clean. She said we were going to be a family and do family things... blah, blah, blah. Those wolf tickets she was selling did not last long enough for the ink to dry on the paper.

The apartment owner and his wife were recovering drug addicts who were tryin' to do better for each other and their two kids. Because they understood Mama's situation, they always allowed Bernard and I to come over and eat. They made breakfast, lunch, and dinner available to us if we wanted, which we did, but Mama told us it was rude and not to take advantage of them. This made us angry. What other choice did we have? It was not like she was doing it for us. Her life was sitting around all day and waiting for the mailman to come, to see if her welfare check had arrived. Her actions depressed me. So in an effort to try and escape the madness, I started to explore the gym and park across the street.

Though I had never participated in organized sports, everyone thought that I should because I was so big. The more time I spent there, the more it allowed me to spend time with Bernard and reflect. We used to talk about my suicidal thoughts,

Mama's dependence on drugs, Benny's desire to help us, but not knowing how, and our dreams – how life was going to be different when we got older. Bernard showed me how to lift weights and play football. I started to realize this was a good way to get my anger out. My days there with Bernard were like physical and mental therapy.

Most days, after school I went to the park or gym with Bernard, then off to pump gas to make money for dinner. Though I had a new found outlet, I still tried to stay away as much as possible. I really thought I was making a change for the better: my behavior at school was improving and I started to try my class work again. Disappointingly, just as I thought things were going smooth, Bernard left and went back to Jeanie's. He told me that he was fed up with Mama and her ways. He said that though he loved being with me, helping me and protecting me, he needed to get away from her. He said Jeanie did not bother him like she did me and that his friends were all in Compton. He knew that these friends shared the same feelings and lifestyle as him and they had grown to be his family. He tried to encourage me to go with him, but I knew that I could not go to hell ever again.

The night Bernard left, I wept and wondered who would be my support system. What would I do?... Who would give me guidance?... Who would counsel me?... I was alone.

Chapter Twenty-One

My insides were bubbling with anger...

Once Mama found out that Bernard had left, she started leaving me alone for long periods of time. She would go off to L.A. to get high and only return to show face and collect her check. She was high all the time. To maintain, I continued to sell my baseball cards to my teacher, Mr. Coleman (who knew about my situation and I believed only bought the cards to ensure I had money to eat). I no longer had Bernard to lean on, Mama was in L.A. and Benny was smoking crack with no hope for taking care of his son. My life began to slide backwards, deeper and deeper into the pit of poverty, anger, and dysfunction.

The plus side to Mama being gone all the time was that I had a lot of time to be on my own. Though I would have preferred Bernard to be there with me, I knew that I was not going to have to deal with her fixes, stealing or highs. I was at peace with this part of living alone. I liked the silence. I did not think Mama would ever leave me alone for longer than a week, but after three weeks had passed, I called Benny and told him Mama had left me. He was furious. He then told me he was going to find her and that she should be home soon. After a month and no sign of Mama, I had to really struggle, and eventually come to grips with the fact that no one cared about me. Though Benny may have felt, or presented like he felt, sorry about the situation, he did not offer to help me. Two months went by and I saw Mama once, which was when she came for her check. She did not speak, she opened the door, snatched the check off the counter and left. I knew she was going to cash it and smoke it away, so I did not even bother asking if she was coming back. This opened my eyes to what she was really capable of and what was important to her. My mission was survival, nothing more nothing less.

After the long commute to and from school, I would go directly to the gas station to earn for money for food. If business was not going well there, I would beg for money. If that did not work I would steal the food as I needed. The only way I knew how to survive was by hussling and I did it well. Most people did not mess with me because I was big. Every once in a while the man in the black Mercedes would come and let me fill-up his tank, giving me $10 or $20 dollar tips. Every time I went to ask him his name or thank him he was gone like a ghost. I did not know who he was but he was a blessing in disguise. Three months had passed and Mama was nowhere to be found. The manager had put an eviction notice on the door which said we had until the end of the month to move out. I figured Mama was not paying the rent, but he probably did not know that she had not been there in months. I got a hold of Benny again to tell him that Mama had not been there in three months and that we were getting evicted. He then offered his room to share with me, but I refused. There was something in me that could not take a hand out from someone

I felt did not genuinely care about me. I knew it would be no different than before and I did not want to go back to that situation.

A few days later, Mama returned. This time she had Junior and his wife with her. From what I could tell Mama was living close to them and together the three of them were getting high. They pooled their government checks together to get more drugs, thus allowing them to get high more often and longer. The three of them came together because Junior had gotten evicted for lack of paying rent and Mama told them they could come to her place. To top it off, Junior's wife was nine months pregnant, though this did not stop her from smoking. The eviction notice on the door did not faze any of them as Mama figured we had a good three more months before the Marshal came to kick us out. This allowed them to squat and smoke without the hassles of others. I was left to stay away for as long as I could to avoid all of them. My welcomed peace was now gone, as I was living with three drug addicts... again.

A few days after their return, Mama woke me up telling me that Junior's wife was having her baby. I did not know what she wanted me to do. I wasn't a doctor, nor did we have a phone to call an ambulance, nor did I want to see. But then I realized they were all too high to even know what to do. So I approached the washroom to see her sitting on the toilet, with the baby in the toilet, umbilical cord still attached. She had given birth and did not even know it because she was so high. The baby was high as well, since she had just finished smoking a half hour before. It was the saddest thing I had ever witnessed. The baby did not cry, but just was limp from the drugs. She removed the cord and sat there as if she had no idea what had just happened or that she had a new born baby in her arms. She had started her own child's life with less brain cells, no prenatal care, nor any ounce of love and affection. With all the commotion, Mama had alerted the neighbors who called the paramedics. When they arrived, Junior's wife did a good job of covering up her high and they never asked. I felt horrible because I knew that child was going to struggle for the next few weeks and after that have to live in a similar situation as me. I hoped she would be placed in foster care like her siblings to at least have a decent shot at a good life.

After this I knew I had to leave. I contemplated running away, but knew it would only be a matter of time before they would leave again. Desperate for money, they left using the baby as a means to beg for money, pulling the sympathy card every chance they had. Though I wanted to call Benny and take him up on his offer, I was too used to being on my own and making my own decisions. I knew that this would make Mama mad, but I did not care. I had rage too. My insides were bubbling with anger at so many people and at so many different levels. Because I needed to be on my own, I decided that before the Marshal came I was going to leave. With that decision firm in my mind, a few days later I packed up my items in one large trash bag and left.

SURVIVAL

Education, education, education,
Go out and get it, 'cause there will soon be liberation.
But what about today?
My mama is on crack; no food in the house, and my hunger grows day by day,
Yet education will eventually set me free.
Let's keep it real
At the age of nine, I have no father figure and my table is missing a meal
Now what options do I face?
Go to school, get an education, and hope my hunger goes away.
Not a chance.
There is no way in hell this book can fill my tummy
I'm not a dummy
Let's keep it real
I'm hungry now, so boxes of cereal I'll steal
Ah that's better
I can now go on
But don't think it's over, cause my hunger still grows strong
What is a child to do?
No mother, no father, so I'll turn to you
Yet you shut me down too
So I'm stranded in the dark
Shut out from Noah's ark
Left to drown in a sea of troubles
With no lifeguard to save my soul.
How bold
You expect me to go to school, when I can't even see the light
And do what's right
What about you leaders who won't even feed us
You expect me to look up to you
When you look down on me

Liberty.
I can't get past my biological needs
Yet you expect me to pass a class and succeed
What is a child to do?
When you have tortured my kind
And blocked us out from the sunshine
Yes, you, the powers that be
Yawl not all white, there is some who even look like me
What a shame
Don't use my life as a game
It's precious
I'm just like you
I was just born into a manifested cycle, called the ghetto
Inequalities petrol, gasoline if you know what I mean.
Let's let the truth surface
You did this for a purpose
As my hunger grows and education I lack
Guided by ignorance and cursed 'cause I'm black
I am supposed to succeed.
You fail to mention I live in a world of greed
So I plead for help
Yet you looked the other direction
Turned your back on me and denied me your protection.
Now the savage in me is free
Guiding me to a biological destiny
Food, clothes, and warm shelter
You begin to look at me as though I was helter skelter
A criminal.
I won't stop cause the hunger goes on
I speak for the youth
You can deny the lie but you can't deny the truth
This is a taste of my reality
Not sugar coated and definitely not a fallacy
This is what you created.

A subculture, alienated, better yet, segregated from the majority
Now just cause you possess the authority, doesn't give you the right to control me
Let's go back to this thing called liberty
A hypocritical meaning that belittles me
It states that every man is free, and equal
Yet it excludes my people
Why lie when the truth is so clear
Is it fear?
Cause the reality is, I can co-exist with you
Have a better life and encourage my kids to see it through
But you think you figured out a way to keep me trapped
You infiltrated my lifestyle and had my phone tapped
So that you can study the way we work
And develop a plan to cause our life style to go berserk
But see I was blessed
God possessed me with this thing called a third eye, so that I can see through this mess
This conflicted mentality that's been implanted in the minds of ghetto youth
Will be eradicated so that they see the truth
It's time to rearrange this blasphemous way of living
So that their minds get free.
It's time to show them the truth, so that they see the opportunity.
The opportunity to escape from this madness and end this sadness that's been going on for centuries
A life style that's sent thousands of our kind to penitentiaries.
But collectively, we can make a change
Now it might sound strange, but we can eradicate this lifestyle that was designed for us
And stop this madness that's been causing a fuss
To that as a people, we rise

Chapter Twenty-Two

22

I got to look at the stars at night...

With nowhere to go, I decided to stay in the park across the street from the apartment. The plan was only for a few days as I could scope out the apartment to wait for the Marshal to come. Once Mama, Junior, his wife and the baby were gone I planned to sneak back in there. My thought was simple: get to school early for breakfast, attend class, have a big lunch, complete school, head to pump gas for dinner money, shower at the gym that Bernard and I hung out at, then hid in the bushes to sleep at night. I was not getting much sleep anyway, so this plan was not too bad. I would put my clothes behind a few trees that were near a building, so no one would mess with them and do the same thing the next day.

This idea was not too bad, except on days when it rained, then I would have to stand under the park shelter and I would not get much sleep. I was content with my situation. I was on my own and no one controlled me. I watched the apartment, just to find that not only had the Marshal evicted Mama and the rest of the family, but they locked off the apartment, so there was no option of me sneaking back in. I was fine with sleeping in the park. I got to look at the stars at night and no one told me what to do. I had a lot of time to think, which fueled my anger for others. My behavior at school was starting to get back in check, but outside of school I was a force to be reckoned with.

There were times when I kept to myself and had a "screw the world" attitude, but most times I was very physically aggressive. This was my means to survive. I thought I had to punk others before they tried to punk me. I would beat up adults to steal from them. Curse out police officers if they were driving by, and then run before they could catch me. Steal from every market, gas station and store I was in. When people looked at me I would swear at them and challenge their position on me. I was plain bad with a capital B-A-D. But my tactics worked. Most people in the neighborhood left me alone and were afraid of my acts. The problem was that over time I got tired of these deviant acts and longed for a "regular life," whatever that was.

After about three months of living in the park and maintaining my survival, I decided that I would be better off living with Benny. I did not know where Mama was, I was not going back to hell, and I had already tried going to stay with Peanut. So I approached the owner of the motel asking him if I could use the phone. He obliged and I called Benny, letting him know I was coming to live with him. The next day I was on the bus to his apartment. I was happy to know that I was going to have a roof over my head.

Chapter Twenty-Three

23

...all I could do was grin from ear to ear, knowing what was coming the next day.

Staying with Benny meant I had a longer commute to and from school. I was going from Inglewood to Long Beach to attend Long Beach Jordan School. Benny was still doing his drug thing and I knew that when he was high I had to avoid him. Being with Benny was not too bad. He cooked for me and there was always food in the refrigerator, like the last time I stayed with him. I never asked him why he called Jeanie, nor did he bring it up. It was hard for me to trust him and after living in the park for three months I had become very suspicious of everyone around me. I hid everything that meant something to me for fear it would get stolen for drugs, money or just to hurt me. Despite his shortcomings and my feelings, I appreciated him for giving me a roof over my head.

As Benny was out a lot getting high, I began to hang around with a guy named Laron. Though he went to a different school, we saw a lot of each other around the neighborhood. We started to spend more time together and before I knew it we were inseparable. Laron wanted to be in a gang and often perpetrated like he was a Blood from San Diego. Though I knew this was probably not the best thing for him to do, I did not mind, it did not affect me because I was not perpetrating anything, my family was deep in the Bloods, so if needed I could call on them. I was in 9th grade and he was in 11th, but because of my size people thought I was older. Though I was bigger, he had more experience committing crimes, which made it easy for him to convince me to commit a felony.

One Sunday night we were bored, so Laron suggested that we steal a car. I did not care about anything, I had avoided the law up until that point, no one worried about me, so I decided why not. I had never driven before, so I was not only curious about obtaining the car, but getting behind the wheel. After searching for a while we ended up at a local sweatshop in downtown L.A. where the graveyard shift employees had already started working. The daring part of the steal had our adrenaline rushing which added to the excitement. I could feel my heart racing and my pulse pounding. I did not know if these physical symptoms were my nerves or excitement that I was about to cruise around the city.

We entered a car near the gate positioning ourselves on the floor. Laron showed me how to break the steering column and snap a pin in the shaft to start the engine. He told me that a screwdriver usually worked better because it was metal and longer. The car started. He hopped in the driver's seat as I climbed into the passenger seat. That was easy enough. We slowly pulled out the sweatshop lot and made our way down the alley to the street. That was easier than I had ever imagined. As we drove around town we scoped out girls and tried to decide if we wanted to get something to eat. As we discussed our options, I could not help but feel eager about stealing our next car. After our L.A. tour I knew I had to return to Inglewood and Laron wanted to go back to Long Beach. Because of this, we decided we would steal another car allowing us both to make it back to our destinations.

We found a car that Laron thought was a good prospect for him and pulled alongside of it. My heart started racing again; the anticipation was filling my bones. I asked Laron if I could do this job and he agreed. Hoping that I was a quick learner, I opened the door, lay on the floor, popped the column and stuck a pin in. The car immediately started up. I smiled with joy as I knew I was never going to have to ride the bus again. What was even more exciting about this theft was that we were right across from the motel which Benny and I stayed in. I did not care. I continued with my Grand Theft Auto ensuring that the car was still running. Laron hopped into the car and headed for home as not to miss his curfew. I ensured the first car was secure for my drive the next morning and ran into the house.

I was so keyed up to drive to school the next day I could hardly focus. Laron did not let me drive the first car we stole, so I still had the anticipation of driving creeping through my bones. As I sat in the motel with Benny, I needed to find out more about driving. I started asking Benny all about cars and driving. I needed to make sure I knew what I was doing the next day. I asked about the controls, the pedals, turning, stopping, everything. He was coming off a high, so he answered willingly and did not think anything about my heavy questioning. He answered in detail not knowing he was an accessory to my theft and driving the next morning. I felt as close as ever to driving without actually being behind the wheel. As I lay in bed that night, all I could do was grin from ear to ear, knowing what was coming the next day.

The next morning Benny woke up at the same time I did. He had to be at work early, but I always left before him because I had to travel further. This was perfect because I could get in the car and take off even before he left the house. I knew that sometimes he watched me as I walked to the bus stop, so I pretended to make my normal trip. When I knew he was not looking any more, I ran to the car, started it up, ducked low to the ground and hit the pedal. Though I did not know much about driving I knew the pedal on the right made the car move. As I cruised the streets, I began to get the hang of driving. It was not difficult, but I did have to work to keep the car in between the lines. Turning was the hardest for me, as the first time I tried I overshot the turn and ran up on the curb. As I relaxed behind the wheel, I was proud of my new accomplishment. Little did I know that my accomplishment (also known as my impulse decision) would ultimately be a huge mistake.

Chapter Twenty-Four

24

*At the very least he was
going to beat the hell out of me...*

Being a balmy morning, the windows fogged up because I had not let the car warm up. As I drove down the street, I wiped the area in front of me and rolled down the driver's side window to see. As the car warmed up the windows cleared and I was rolling. I turned up the radio, "I Wanna Sex You Up" blasted from the speakers. Not wanting to look too suspicious I rolled down the other three windows while stopped at a stop light to ensure the busted window in the back did not give me away. As I sang to the music and continued down the street I did not notice the police lights flashing in my rearview mirror, nor could I hear the sirens or the cop on his intercom, as Color Me Badd drowned them out. I was on a mission and would not have stopped if it was not for the motorcycle cop who cut in front of me forcing me to slam on the brakes.

My joy immediately turned to pure fear. My heart nearly jumped out of my throat. Part of me wanted to run, but as I looked around, I saw that the car was surrounded with at least four cop cars. I wanted to try, but I knew that if I did not get away I would be in more trouble. The cops ordered me to get out of the car with my hands in the air. They told me to get on my knees. As I opened the door I could see guns drawn with barrels pointing right at me as though I was one of America's Most Wanted. I was petrified and regretted not trying to make a run for it when I had my chance. As I kneeled on the ground one officer approached me. Once he got to me, he pushed my upper body to the ground and placed his knee in my neck, pressing my face to the concrete as additional officers came in and put the hand cuffs on me.

Once cuffed they started with a borage of questions: "What's your name? Where did you get this car? Who was with you when you stole it? Where were you going? How old are you?" I was bombarded with questions and did not know how to answer. I said, "I'm 14." They laughed and did not believe me. I guess my size had finally caught up with me. As one officer continued to laugh he told me that if I really was 14, I should be playing football and be in school. I explained that I lived two hours from school and that I was heading there. They then realized I was telling the truth, picked me up, put me in the cop car and carted me off to the precinct.

Being a minor they could not book me, so they called Benny. After I knew they were going to call him, I asked if they could put me in a foster home instead of releasing me to him. I was truly scared of what he was going to do to me. At the very least he was going to beat the hell out of me and I did not want to face him nor his reaction. I was trying to think of ways I could run from him, as I knew this would be my best option if they were going to release me into his custody. I figured that he would not beat me in front of the cops and if I darted away, I might avoid the wrath of his fist to my face.

When Benny did arrive I could see the disgust in his face. He kept saying to me,
"I don't believe you played me like that, asking me all those questions about driving and then stealing a car. I wondered why you were asking, but didn't give it a second thought." As we exited the station he continued to talk to himself and became so irritated that he reached over to clock me, but quickly remembered where he was. For a split second I thought he was going to beat my ass right in front of the police. Outside the station my aunt was waiting for us. She had given Benny a ride to the station. The ride back to the motel was a quiet one. Once there Benny instructed me to stay there until he returned from work.

As the hours passed, I considered leaving, but I really had nowhere to go. I did not want to get beat because I knew I would snap, but I knew I had to face my consequences. When Benny got home, surprisingly he did not lay one finger on me. He yelled and yelled and yelled but did not beat me. The end result was a strict punishment until my court date a month later, which meant nothing, as the fact remained that he was not around much. I just had to make sure I was home when he was home. Unfortunately, a month later I missed my court date which caused a lot of problems.

Benny started using very heavily again and I ended up getting locked up for missing court. They sentenced me for a week in juvenile hall. This was the worst experience I had ever had… worse than living on the streets, with Jeanie or with Mama and everyone else. I had no soap or comb, and the first two days I was there I could not shower. I was there with kids who were staying much longer than me, so they had nothing to lose when it came to confrontations, behaviors, and attitudes. I quickly figured out that the people who did not care if they lived or died were the most dangerous people in the world. I had never categorized myself as one of these types of people, but in the eyes of everyone else, I was just like the rest of them.

Having been on my own for so long without rules or anyone telling me what to do, this week was extremely hard for me. I had to listen to whatever the correctional officers said, dress a certain way and walk a certain way. When moving around the facility we had to walk with our hands behind our backs, with the right hand over the left. Any nonconformity... we were immediately sent to our rooms for the rest of the day. I wanted my freedom back. I did not ever want to come back to this place. I realized the joy of freedom and never wanted that taken away. The week could not have gone any slower, but the day came when I was released to Benny. He really did not seem to care that I had just spent the past week locked up. Being 14, I realized that the institution was designed to keep those who had no escape impoverished. It was a means to entrap people like me in the clutches of life in the ghettos. I did not want that and knew I was never going to steal another car if it caused me to go back there.

Benny took me to the motel and left to go get high. I knew he wanted me gone again and it was only a matter of time before he was going to kick me out. Three days later he came home and told me he had lost his job. Because my troubles caused him to have to take so many days, his boss chose to lay him off with cutbacks. He told me he was going to live with his sister and that I was going to have to go back to live with Jeanie. He was spiraling out of control and blaming me. I did not want to go back to Jeanie's as she was already bitter towards my family, especially me. The only reason she would let me stay with her was to rub it in my face that I "needed" her. I would have been content living back in the park, but because the court had to keep tabs on me, I knew I was going to have to endure her hell one more time.

FACTS

Nigga not, killa not, steela not,

But what do we got.

We got all odds against us.

We raised to learn not to trust,

We're born into a world of stress.

And we focus on petty things like how to dress.

We're taught to beware of our own kind,

Not to use our mind, and continue to be blind.

But the cold thing is, we don't even know.

We are like chickens with their heads cut off, and don't have nowhere to go.

Where is our sense of direction?

I want you to step back and take a look at your reflection.

Now tell me what do you see,

It's crazy cause your reflection tells you, you don't even know where you want to be.

But see, you not worried about that

You worried about watching your back, selling your crack,

And how much money you can stack.

But see, that can only get you so far,

Yea, it might get you a car

And to them young innocent ghetto kids, might look at you as a star.

But only time will tell when I see your black ass riding around in the back seat of a police car

Open your eyes, you see how the system work,

Got you riding around looking like a jerk,

And at the same time got you thinking this is just work.

But on the flip side,

I'll show you how to ride, and at the same time not have to hide.

Brotha we can do this together

And have a brotherhood that can last forever.

It ain't too late to be who you want to be,

See what you want to see,

Brotha don't give way to defeat,

Be so eager to retreat.

Look at your reflection.

Respect yourself

And have the courage to walk in a new direction.

    Because the struggle continues.

Chapter Twenty-Five

I would not stop, fist after fist, in his face...

Returning to Jeanie's was hell, just like I thought it would be. The only plus was being with Bernard again. We regularly shot the breeze and talked about getting out of there. He promised me that after he graduated from high school and got on his feet he would let me come stay with him. He knew how unhappy I was and that I needed some type of hope to sustain. Being with Bernard allowed those around the neighborhood to associate me with him, rarely did people pick on me, but soon there was a hit out on me because of Bernard's association with the Bloods. This hit did not bother me, because in the back of my mind, I could take anyone who approached me.

About a month after we started attending school together, people started threatening Bernard's life, both in and out of school. Soon, Bernard started carrying a gun to school every day.

He was never shy about carrying a gun or his ability to use it if he had to. I knew he was serious and with no hesitation would go down in a blaze of gunfire if a rival gang member tried to do something to him or me. I knew that I could hold my own, so it did not bother me that the threats increased, until one day at lunch it all came to a head.

While eating and minding our own business a rival gang member came up to Bernard and started talking mess, real loud. He wanted us to meet him behind the school to fight. This was nothing but a word to me. I was ready and willing. Not realizing that it might be a trap for something bigger than just a fist to fist fight, Bernard pulled me back telling me to wait. He then told the guy that he would meet him in front of the school. I did not understand, but because Bernard was older and streetwise I listened. Later that day we stood outside the front of the school, posed like statues waiting for even the smallest thing to pop off. We waited and waited, nothing happened. Letting the fact that I felt we had intimidated the rival gang member go to my head I boosted that "I knew they weren't gonna do nothing."

The threats continued, until about a week later Bernard did not come to school with me. I continued with my routine as the threats against me persisted. They did not bother me, but day in and day out Bernard begged me not to go to school, it was like he knew something bad was going to happen. I ignored him because school was my solitude. I could not imagine staying at home with Jeanie all day to hear her obnoxious voice, nagging and complaining. I certainly did not need her abuse towards me. I continued on my trips to school, which crossed over gang territories. The Crips regularly rode the bus with me and knew who I was. For the most part I minded my own business while they harassed me, until one day I had enough.

Riding on the bus was my peace. As I sat there four Crips got on the bus and immediately started with me. They threatened me, harassed me, and did everything they could to provoke me to get into it with them. I simply ignored them for the majority of the trip, until they threatened to kill Bernard. I saw red. I could not control it anymore. I went from zero to 100 in a millisecond. I stood up, went over to one of them who was seated in the middle of the bus and repeatedly punched him in his face. I would not stop, fist after fist, in his face, his nose, his eyes, punch after punch, blood was flying everywhere. I continued. People were yelling at me to stop before I killed him. I continued. The bus driver and the three other Crips pulled me off of him. His face was full of blood, eyes closed shut and he was unconscious. I was kicked off the bus, two blocks from school. As I walked to school I felt no remorse, no pain and no fear. I almost had a slight grin on my face. He got what he deserved.

When I got to school, word of the incident on the bus had traveled faster than lightening. As I entered the school a hush came over the corridor and the Principal beckoned me to his office. He escorted me to the back of the school and quickly encouraged me to get home as fast as I could. I was expelled almost immediately. The school officials feared what would happen to me if I continued there. After my expulsion they sent me to a school even further away. Ironically the bus stop that I had to wait for the bus was directly across from the school that had just expelled me. The ride was even longer. Two hours. My new trip meant that while everyone else was sleeping I was riding the bus to school. But to me it didn't matter, it just meant more time away from Jeanie. I never thought about my actions or being expelled; he shouldn't have threatened my brother.

My new high school, Lakewood, was a lot safer than my old one and they had a better education to offer me. Lakewood was predominantly white, but there were enough of us to make me feel comfortable. I quickly became acquainted with a few black people who welcomed me with open arms. No one knew of my expulsion and I left it like that. When asked why I transferred, I just simply explained that my Mama wanted a change. The school was intriguing to me because all different cultures hung with each other. Though most groups were dominated by one culture there was always someone else with them. There were unspoken boundaries between the groups and I respected this culture. For the most part the students left me alone and I did the same. I became relaxed and content with my new school pretty fast. Little did I know that my time there was about to come to an abrupt end.

Chapter Twenty-Six

26

"Son you know what this means."

Though the majority of the black kids hung together, there were a few who made the decision to hang with other crowds. There was one black guy, an 11th grader, who's family was from an affluent neighborhood he regularly boosted and bragged about what he had, what he could buy and how he was better than everyone. I ignored him because to me these kinds of guys have nothing but fluff and hot air to back up what they said. What he possessed did not matter to me, nor did I care. I guess my size and demeanor regularly pissed him off. Every time he saw me he would say,
"Just because you're big, doesn't mean that I can't and won't kick your ass." I never engaged in his silliness, nor tried to get physical with him because I realized that his personal insecurities overpowered his ability to think logically. He tried every method he could to push my buttons, thinking that because he was a little

bit taller than me he could keep running his mouth. He did not know me, nor my background or my anger issues. I knew he could not kick my ass and so did he. He was nothing but smoke and screens, and I did not want to be part of his show. I knew that if I got into a fight, my track record would speak for itself and I would be kicked out, so I continued with school and made every attempt to ignore him.

I did a pretty good job of ignoring him until the day when he put his hands on me. In my mind he could talk trash as much as he wanted as long as he did not touch me. Then it happened.

We were all hanging out as a group and he approached us, immediately tormenting me about my clothes and my style. This was a battle I had fought my entire life so his word to me were bouncing off me like a rubber ball. As he went by, he pushed the back of my head and told me I dressed like a bum. That was a big mistake on his part. I pretended like the push in the back of the head did not faze me, when in actuality it had lit a fire under me so hot the devil was running. I turned around, looked him in the face, locked eyes with him and started to laugh. He thought I was laughing at his joke, so he started to laugh. Then out of nowhere, POW, I hit him directly in his face. He looked at me in shock. I had shown no facial expression when I hit him and continued to look him in his face. He became completely enraged, but this is exactly what I wanted. I wanted him to see red and try as hard as he could to fight me, since that's what he was boosting. I knew his emotion would control his fight rather than his mind. I was in complete control of my anger and knew what to do with it.

He rushed me; I stepped to the side and punched him again in the same place. He turned around and tried again, and again I punched him in the face. You could see him trying to regroup and reassess the situation to try and kick my ass.

The determination was written all over his face and a large portion of the student body was watching. He could not lose after all that talk and to a freshman. I smiled, which frustrated him more. As his attempts continued to fail, my punches got harder and harder. Eventually he was on the ground balled up in a fetal position as I continued to pummel him. The reality of his talk for the past few weeks was coming to light, I kicked his ass. Period.

As security came to stop me, I looked around to see that the circus had become entertainment to the rest of the school. We were sent to the office and once the Principal saw it was me; he shook his head and said,
"Son you know what this means." I knew that this fight meant I was expelled, but he deserved it and I did not feel bad. The only thing I felt bad about was that I was going back to the ghetto where as the Principal said, "I belonged."

I WANT TO GROW

Can I grow to be what I desire?
Can my dreams become realities, or do I have to continue to burn in ghetto's fire?
Can I reach for the stars and as far as the outer space,
Or am I trapped in ghetto's cage and forced to live in disgrace?
Can my dreams travel outside the 'hood,
Or am I forced to submit to crime because you told me there was no way I could?
Can I become a lawyer, an educator, or even the president of the United States,
Or should I give up and let the 'hood determine my fate?
Can I break the barriers that lock me in,
Or should I just give up like my friend?
Is it possible for me to break this norm,
Or are the rains too powerful for me to make it from the storm?
Should I go to school in hopes that it creates a path,
Or should I fall to my knees and submit to ghettos wrath?
What should I do?
Been in the 'hood for so long I forgot the skies were blue,
Black rains have plagued my kind and me for centuries,
Got us thinking our lives are empty.
I want to grow
I want to soar
I want to explore the corners of the earth, and be released from

this life so poor.
I want to be free,
I want to be me,
A human being that controls his destiny.
I want to raise my child away from this land of crime,
I want to make sure that my child doesn't wind up doing time.
I want to defy the odds inflicted on us.
I want to live in a land where I can trust.
I will find that place,
That land of opportunity where I am not hated because of my face.
I will pave the way for my child.
Why should he have to live like an animal in the wild?
I will be the keeper of hope,
The key that unlocks poverty's gate, so my seeds don't have to grow up around dope.
I will rise,
Bringing with me my people, so that they no longer have to hide.
I will be that light that has been burnt out in the ghetto since the beginning.
I will make sure we are winning.
I will grow,
Let's rise my seeds.

Chapter Twenty-Seven

...it gave me a chance to really think...

I knew the worst part of my second expulsion in less than two months, was the fact that I was going to have to tell Jeanie. As soon as Jeanie found out that I had been expelled from another school she immediately threw it in my face,
"You're nothing but a screw-up. You will never amount to anything just like the rest of your no good family." She was highly pissed. She told me that I was a bad influence on her kids and that I had to go. Home to home, school to school, no one wanted me; no one cared about me... The story of my life.

I happily accepted the news and called Benny, hoping that he had become stable since living with his sister. He told me that he was now living with his girlfriend Sharon and that she thought it would be fine for me to come and live with them. As I rode the bus to my father's, it gave me a chance to really think about my life and where I was headed. Maybe Jeanie was right. I was a screw up and I was not going to amount to anything. My life was screwed up from the start and I continued the pattern that Mama and Benny had set for me. How many more schools was I going to get kicked out of? Mama did not care about me. Peanut was locked up. Bernard was banging hard since he dropped out and Travie was content living in that hell hole with Jeanie. I was left to use this chance with Benny as a new beginning for my future. I sat back in the seat of the bus and knew things this time were going to be different. This was going to be the turning point in my life.

I thought the difference was going to be good, instead I arrived to a similar hell as the one I just left. Sharon was just as bad as Jeanie. She was Satan's spawn disguised in Jesus paraphernalia. She claimed to be a Christian and even went to first service on Sunday. Yet after those two hours of sanctifying and praising the Lord, she returned home to unleashed wickedness. She was like a hungry wolf on an innocent pack of deer. She complained about everything and was angry all the time. She wanted things her way, but did not seem to have enough ambition to manage the things she wanted to control. She had two daughters who were just as coo-coo as she was. Her one daughter, Aretha, was my age, 14, and had a baby. She was pregnant again and was the most arrogant girl I had ever met. She did what she pleased, when she pleased because she knew that her sister and her mama would take care of her baby. Unfortunately the other daughter, Sharmony, was following down the same path because she looked up to her big sister.

Sharon did whatever her daughters wanted her to do, which made for uneasiness in my mind. Sharmony was used to getting her way and at 13 if she did not get her way she would throw tantrums to drive everyone insane until she got what she wanted. Benny was rarely around because he had a new job and wanted to do right by Sharon. I could not relate to anyone in the house so I kept to myself. Needless to say I realized that living there, like everywhere else, I was going to have to stay away for as long as I could each night; just using it as a place to sleep. I knew that school was going to have to be my positive. I had been kicked out of two schools in the first semester of my freshmen year, so my new school, Thomas Jefferson, was going to have to be my clean slate. I told myself that I was not going to get into trouble, but instead stay there until graduation... Assuming I made it that far.

The staff at Jefferson welcomed me with open arms. I quickly realized that I was in a place that maybe someone cared about me. Before getting kicked out of Lakewood, I had been talking to the football coach about joining the team. I got the idea from my junior high PE teacher (and the police after my botched car theft) and decided to investigate some more. Now that I was at Jefferson, I figured I could tryout and at least get in the weight room like Bernard had taught me. So on the first day I arrived to practice, walked out on the field and realized that as a freshman I was bigger than everyone. After a few hits I loved it. There was nothing like hitting someone with all your force, standing up after it and not getting suspended or expelled for it. After a few practices I felt like I had a new family. Football was good for me; it was nothing more than an easy way for me to let out my pinned up aggression and a constructive way to stay away from home. I also met a new friend, Isaac, Ike for short. He seemed nice enough and from what I saw had a pretty good head on his shoulders.

After football, I went home to my room, closed the door, came out for dinner then went back in my room. I did not have much homework to do as the academics at Jefferson were a joke, the material that we were taught had nothing to do with us, our culture or our lifestyle. They did not understand that gang bangers from South Central could care less about Mozart, The Berlin Wall or Physics. My teachers were all crazy, but it was funny. Ms. Fadler came to class in a frantic panic. She would try and teach a lesson, but was barely understood because she had a speech impediment and ate while teaching. She appeared to be a crack head, as her mannerisms matched those of crack heads I had seen strung out and her body language was like she was high. After about a month of her shenanigans she ended up putting the directions on the board and going back to her office. She never monitored our class, nor graded work; there were always extra credit options for the students who took that responsibility from her.

One evening after a long day of football, I came home to Sharmony having sex on the floor in front of my bedroom door. I ignored them and went in my room to find that it had been torn apart, and with many of my clothes were missing. As I walked passed them on the floor again in pure disgust and anger, I noticed a duffle bag by the door. I opened it to find that Sharmony had stolen my clothes to give to her boyfriend. I guess the sex was his way of thanking her. Instead of confronting her, knowing that Sharon would just take her side, I retrieved my articles, went back to my room, found a pad lock and knew from then on when I was gone I would lock my door. I was starting to see that I had nothing in common with these people, except animosity, which would get me nowhere. Benny was not around and I knew I was on my own to try and make something from this hell of a life I was living.

Chapter Twenty-Eight

I just hoped Benny would not mess this great thing up.

As time progressed, there were three things that were consistent in my life: football, no academic rigor, and Benny arguing with Sharon. It was a shame that I did not learn anything in the classroom, but I continued to be eligible to play, which was all I cared about. Ike and I ran the school, though we were underclassmen. Ms. Fadler got fed up with our obnoxious behavior in class and kicked us out for the entire semester. We never tried to get back in the class nor did any administrator come looking for us. When report cards came out we had B's so we did not sweat it. I had found my place at Jefferson and knew that as long as I stayed under the radar things would be fine.

About mid-year, I came home to find Benny sitting in the living room with a bag. He and Sharon had broken up because he was stealing from her to buy drugs. I was devastated. Though

Sharon and her children were horrible, I liked Jefferson and my routine and did not want to give it up. Crack had foiled my plans again. I looked at him in resentment and asked him what we were going to do. Benny explained that all this time he had been with Sharon and he had a girlfriend on the side. He went on to explain that they were getting a home together in Compton and that's where we were going to stay. My only concern was staying at Jefferson. He told me that I would be able to continue there if I wanted, though the bus ride would be a little longer.

Happy by the news, I ran up to my room, unlocked the door and started packing my clothes. Aretha came in asking what I was doing. I quickly responded, "We're outta this hell hole." She looked puzzled. Then she realized I was packing up so that we could move out. She ran to her mother and asked who was going to take care of her kids. They were never my responsibility and now that she was pregnant for a third time, I was glad to leave her madness, Sharmony's drama, and Sharon's anger. About ten minutes later I emerged from the hall with my stuff, smiled as we walked out the door and headed for Compton to live with Renee'.

I did not realize that I knew Renee'. She had been around a few times when we were young. I could remember her buying us clothes so we did not have to rotate between the four of us. I also recalled her cooking great meals. Benny seemed to like her then, but I never knew what their relationship was. To us she was just a nice lady who Benny knew. Now I knew what was really up back then. Thinking back, she was probably the nicest lady I knew so seeing her again brought a huge grin to my face. She seemed excited to see me as well. When we came in she told me she had a surprise for me. She had set up a room for me and in the corner was a glass aquarium with a snake inside. I had never been so happy in my life.

Many years before I had asked her to get me a snake, but she was afraid so did not oblige. Because I did not live with her, she told me maybe one day. The day had come. She wanted to make sure I was happy and comfortable in my new home. I felt like God was winking at me. I had made a positive decision to try and stay out of trouble and he was winking at me letting me know I was on the right track. I just hoped Benny would not mess this great thing up. I looked at him and let him know that I approved and sat on my bed holding the snake, hoping that if I was dreaming no one would ever wake me up.

ào•œ

With things at home looking up, school easier than ever and football, I believed my cloudy days had turned to sunshine. One of our coaches, Coach Johnson, let Ike and I come to his house every other week to do lawn work. He knew our situations at home weren't the best, so he did what he could to try and put money in our pockets to help ensure we had the bare necessities. In my mind I think he did it to try and steer us away from selling drugs. He was one of the few staff members who knew the realities of where we lived and what we faced every day. Soon Coach Johnson was like a mentor. He was like the father I never had. He told us that he would do everything in his power to ensure we graduated. I felt like I was his adopted son; eating dinner, getting homework help, having "man" talks, and knowing that I could count on him. Though my past did not fully allow me to trust adults, if there was any adult I was going to trust it was him.

One afternoon after a particularly hard practice, as I was preparing to go home, Coach Johnson pulled me aside. He indicated that he had read through my file and needed to show me something. Open to most of the things he had to say I listened and walked with him down to the practice field. He told me to place my things on the bench and walk to the far end zone. As I listened I thought he might have wanted to teach me a new block or isolation move. I did wonder why he had waited until I had changed into my street clothes, but thought nothing of it. As we stood in the end zone, Coach told me to lay down on the ground and roll myself to the far end zone, 100 yards away. I looked at him like he was crazy. He looked back and in a harsh voice exclaimed,

"ROLL." Not questioning his motives, I began to roll. As I rolled he stood there and watched me get dirt all over my clothes, my face, my hair... everywhere.

"I want you to continue to roll 1,000 yards." As I rolled I became dizzy. I could feel my blood start to boil as I became covered in dirt from the top of my head to the bottom of my shoes. Not that my clothes or appearance were the best, but I did like to try and keep what I had clean, cause I never knew what was going to happen at home. After my 1,000 yards I stopped, stood up and looked at Coach in disgust.

"What was that for?" I asked in a semi-angered tone. Coach Johnson responded,

" I read through your file today and saw your history. I want you to know that you will have plenty of tumbles in life which will cause you to roll, get dirty and even sometimes split your knee. But the true test of a person is not the tumble, the roll or the dirt, but how they recover. Will they continue to roll or will they get up, clean themselves off and continue to walk with their head high? You have had plenty of tumbles in life, I am now challenging you to either continue to roll in the dirt or to get up and walk with your head high." Coach Johnson then left the field in silence.

I watched him march all the way back into the school as I stood alone on the field full of dirt. I had nothing to say.

I understood what he was telling me and knew I had a choice. I picked up my bag, and walked towards the bus stop full of dirt. I did not brush myself off, I was proud of the dirt. As I walked I smiled and my head was as high as it had ever been.

꙰•꙰

At the start of my sophomore year, football started with a new coach. Though Coach Johnson was still there, Coach Chapel joined the team. He had joined the Jefferson staff and wanted to work with us in the weight room. Coach Chapel was a man in his mid-50s but seemed to have the body and spirit of a 20-something year old man. He would lift with us, scrimmage with us and even mess around on the basketball court. Outside of sports, Coach Chapel was a man of business. He was rich. He came to school in three piece suits and drove a Rolls Royce. I did not know what he did to get all that money, but I needed to know. After our first scrimmage of the season he took our team to his house in Palace Verdi, an expensive high end suburb up in the hills. His home was amazing: rooms for days, ocean views and a six car garage. This was the life I wanted to live one day.

"Coach Chapel, How did you get this?" I asked like a naive child. He smiled and replied.

"I buy houses, fix them up and then sell them for a profit. There is always money out there to make, but you have to be willing to work for it and work hard. I found out real estate was where you will never lose and made a business of it." I did not know what all that meant, but I was going to figure it out.

A few days later Coach Johnson and Coach Chapel approached me after practice. I did not know what I had done, but I hoped it was not bad as I did not want to disappoint either one of them. They told me that they wanted me to try and take classes that would prepare me for college. College?... I thought in my head. I knew that I was not going to have money for that, nor did I have the skills and no one I knew even went to college. Mama and Benny did not even graduate from high school. I always knew if I just graduated from high school, I was ahead of the game. They mentioned something about humanities, but I did not know what that was. It sounded like something boring. I barely listened to what they were saying as I contemplated just saying no. As they continued on, I realized that they were telling me this to help me. I did not know if I could trust them, but I knew that they saw something in me. I had to respect them for all they had done for me and I decided that I could at least give it a try. I agreed, and Coach Johnson, being the Dean, said he would talk to my counselor to get my schedule changed. I did not know what I was getting myself into, but it could not have been any worse than anything else I had encountered in my first 15 years.

Chapter Twenty-Nine

29

---
*This would ensure I had
enough money to survive...*

I soon learned that Humanities was a unified course which incorporated English, science, history and politics. It was not going to be too bad, I hoped. The teacher told us that the class would have a lot of guest speakers come in to talk about their jobs and how the different areas of Humanities fit into their daily lives. I figured that would be fine because that meant less work in class, which meant less work out of class. Good. A few weeks into the class our first guest speaker arrived, her name was Debra Constance. She worked at Jon Douglas Real Estate agency, which immediately sparked my interest because of what Coach Chapel had told me about making money.

During her lecture I drifted in and out of paying attention because I just wanted to know how to make money like Coach. At the end of her presentation she encouraged us to go to hear Mr.

Douglas himself speak at our school the following day. This was right up my alley. I needed to hear from the real estate man himself on how to be rich. As luck had it Coach Johnson pulled me in his office the next period asking me to escort Mr. Douglas around the next day. He explained that though Mr. Douglas had agreed to speak, he was apprehensive about the neighborhood. He said that I would be a good person to escort him around because everyone knew who I was and probably would not mess with him when he was with me. I had nothing better to do with my time, so I agreed.

The next day Mr. Douglas arrived at the school. To my surprise he looked awfully familiar pulling up in a black two door Mercedes. As I showed him around the school he explained that he had humble beginnings and had to work hard to get what he had. He told me that being a multi-million dollar real estate company owner, with offices across southern California was very time consuming, but also profitable. All I could think about was money, money, money. I had to get a piece of the real estate game, whatever that was. As we continued to talk he seemed like a genuinely nice man, who wanted to help others. As I listened to his lecture on setting and achieving your goals, I could only imagine being rich and living in a home with an ocean view like Coach Chapel. He was sparking my imagination of all the possibilities that could be if I just had money.

After his lecture Mr. Douglas shadowed me in a few classes. He amazed me. Here was this rich middle-aged white man in the inner city telling high school students never to give up, set high standards for ourselves and work hard to achieve our goals. It was strange, but I was thankful that I got the chance to meet and talk with him. At the end of the day as I walked Mr. Douglas to his car, he thanked me for being his chaperone for the day. I thanked him for sharing his story and time with me. He got in his car, dropped the top and pulled away. As I walked to football practice I was no longer dumbfounded why Mr. Douglas visited to Jefferson. He had struggled at an early age and wanted to give his knowledge to others so they did not make the same mistakes he made when he was younger.

A week after his visit I got a small card from Mr. Douglas. He thanked me for taking the time out of my day to give him a tour and allowing him to shadow me. He included a business card and indicated that if I ever needed him to contact him. I felt that he was a legitimately nice man and that I was privileged to have met and talked with him. He had influenced me in ways he would never know... He gave me the desire to work hard and not use my obstacles as an excuse, but a motivator.

ࢀ•ࣰ

About a month after Mr. Douglas came to Jefferson, I was desperate for a job. I had looked everywhere and no one wanted to hire me. The first school break was coming up and I knew that I needed something to keep me occupied. Coach Johnson encouraged me to reach out to Mr. Douglas as he too had received a letter from him indicating how impressed he was with me. Though hesitant to ask, I decided to call. Upon speaking to Mr. Douglas he indicated that he would find me a position in the office where he worked as he wanted to bring me under his wing. He told me to arrive on my first day out of school, giving me the address to the office. Excited about the opportunity I knew this would be great, though I was going to have to ride the bus four hours each way to get there.

With the addition of my new position at Jon Douglas, I was offered a position at Taco Bell. I decided to work at Jon Douglas during the day and work the graveyard shift at Taco Bell.

This would ensure I had enough money to survive as well as some additional money to trick off. Taco Bell was a no brainer to me, so I used it as work experience. Jon Douglas, on the other hand, was a new role model for me, I got to see things beyond Compton and South Central. My position allowed me to see the outside world. I was like a lion that had been released from his cage. I learned how to escape the confines of the ghetto. This was my first taste of "real" life and I wanted more. I knew that if Coach Johnson and Chapel were right about this college thing, I was going to at least try, but only if the result meant that I could experience the life I saw while working with Jon Douglas.

The work at Jon Douglas was consistently changing. I worked in the corporate offices, assisting in departments that needed help with getting their daily routine done. I helped order supplies with the secretaries, check financial records with the accounting department, worked with the advertising department running ads, learning how they pushed ads in local papers as well as running payroll equipment. I soon learned that I was able to do everything my boss could do, just as long as I watched and learned. This was incredible. As I spoke with Linda, my boss, I found out she had a college degree and made $45,000 a year. I knew that was way more than anyone in my family had ever made, or even thought about making. I also knew that the government was not giving out checks like hers, so I started plotting. I needed to figure out a way to get to the next level to earn a degree, just as Coach Johnson had said.

Chapter Thirty

30

*I had not ever thought
more than a second about it...*

After working a few weeks, I started to compare my two positions. I was getting paid less at Taco Bell but doing more work, while at Jon Douglas I was getting paid more and the work was not nearly as hard or labor intensive. I also saw that when it came to learning new skills and applying it to the work place, I was quicker than people twice my age at Jon Douglas. So one day, while on the bus, I asked myself one question: Which position do you want to have in ten years: one with no opportunity, harder work, in a dangerous setting or one with room for advancement, not as labor intensive, in a comfortable setting? The answer was simple to me.

Soon after answering this question I came to the decision to quit Taco Bell and concentrate solely on Jon Douglas. I figured I might be able to get overtime and additional responsibilities.

For the first time in my life I felt like I had a destination in life, a means to get there and control over what happened. Jon Douglas was an escape for me and as long as I worked there during my school vacations, I knew that I could escape the poverty, drugs, gangs, death and unending cycle of government funded leeches. The more I worked there, the more I thought about the college thing and how, if I could get accepted, I was going to pay for it. No one, not Mama, Junior, Benny, Jeanie, no one, was gonna stop me. I had finally seen that "light" that everyone had talked about for so many years and I knew that that light would take me to new places. As I thought about it more, I decided that with the help of Coach Johnson and Coach Chapel, I was going to use football as my ticket out.

Things were going well, until about six months after we moved in with Renee', Benny started using heavily again. Renee' and I would sit waiting long hours for him to come home. She would say,
"I can't take much more of your father and his behavior, I just can't trust him." I did not want her to leave, and I knew if she was gone I would, for the first time, miss somebody who was alive. A lot of people had left me in my life and I had not ever thought more than a second about it, but I knew if she were to leave (because of her kind heart, being responsible for showing me happiness at home and her unconditional love) I knew I would long to have her back. I understood why she wanted to leave because if I had the chance to escape the drugs that plagued my life, I would have left too. Eventually Benny started stealing money from her too Renee' immediately said she was not going to put up with this behavior, packed up her furniture and left.

I was devastated, because deep down inside I hoped that Benny would marry her. There was something in my mind that thought because he had a good woman he would keep himself clean...she was supportive, kind, and a wonderful first-rate woman...but instead, with her departure he slipped into his habit even more. He told me he did not like the fact that she earned more money than him and his way of rebelling was to use drugs. A crack head will say anything to justify their usage. Renee did give me her number and told me to keep in touch and to let her know if I needed anything. She was a mother to me, and she was gone forever and now my life at home had reverted back to a nightmare, almost immediately.

I tried to stay away as much as possible consuming my life with work at Jon Douglas and focusing on my ideas about college. Things at home with Benny got no better, but Bernard came to live with us, which made me happy. I loved him being around. He was like my sounding board and I was his. We got to spend a lot of time together before all the chaos and now it was me and him again. Bernard's educational career was solid until junior high school, when gangs, moving around and a few deviant acts led him to attend a correctional school. I had looked up to him and hoped that even with attending this correctional school he would graduate and go off to college so that he could tell me how it was.

As Bernard and I grew closer and closer, Benny's habit got worse and worse with his intensity escalating to an all time high... no pun intended. He smoked up the rent money and we were about to get evicted. Soon it was like we were living with Mama. We were hiding our money, staying out late working and avoiding him at all costs. My concentration on football increased, as I knew I was getting better. I got a laptop from the high school counselor to try and help me type papers for Humanities and so

Bernard could work on other activities for his senior year. This was the most expensive item I had ever had, which made me very excited and nervous. I wanted to take care of it and keep it for as long as I could because I did not know if I would ever have another computer. We hid the laptop under the bed, but Benny found it and sold it for drugs. Deep down inside I knew that he was going to take it. I was not too angry, but more disappointed because I thought Benny was different than Mama.

As we came closer to eviction, we started plotting about what we were going to do once we had to move. The day we had our concrete plan, Mama showed up with Travie. Of course she was not there to see how we were, or to show concern, she was there because she needed something. She had gotten herself mixed up in a food stamp selling scheme. She would go to Vegas and sell food stamps for money and needed Bernard for protection from some people who were looking for her. Benny did not want Bernard to go because he was already in a correctional school and could not miss any days. His decision made Bernard really angry.

"You don't deserve to be our father," he proclaimed.

"You steal from us and buy drugs with the money." I was shocked. I had never seen Bernard fly off the handle like that; it was usually me that lost my temper. I could not say anything, but Mama surely did.

"Yeah, Benny you can go to hell because they are my kids." Now I was twice as shocked. Her kids? This coming from a woman who left me for months to survive on my own, did not care that I was living in a park, did not feed me, clothe me or even call to make sure I was alive... Her kids. Wow! I had heard it all.

"Why did you steal our laptop?" Bernard yelled, with anger. I could see the hate in his eyes.

"I did not steal it." Benny said with a smirk on his face that really told the truth. This made Bernard enraged.

Mama chimed in,

"How dare you steal my baby's computer, you thieving bastard." Benny had had enough with the interaction and especially Mama's two cents. He quickly approached her and pushed her with all his force knocking her to the ground. Bernard pushed Benny to defend Mama, and then the fight broke out.

Benny rushed Bernard and Bernard punched Benny dead in the face. Fist started flying left and right. Though I thought I should step in to help break it up, I almost smiled as I watched because for once it was not me who was angry, fighting or rebelling. As the punches slowly ended I could see that Bernard had gotten the best of Benny. This did not sit well with him. He went inside and got a steel baseball bat. Travie screamed frantically at me to stop the fight. He feared the worse, so did I, but I just sat perched on the car, watching the events unfold.

Bernard ran and Benny quickly followed. I could see that Travie was mad at me for not doing anything, but I was not going to chase after them and give the neighbors even more of a show, and quite frankly I just did not, nor could not, care anymore. I was fed up with the shenanigans that my family, especially Benny and Mama, had fed me over the past fifteen years. I only had a few more years to live by their rules which really did not matter anyway. Whatever happened to them was on them. I had no sympathy for them, they put me through hell and they had (and deserved) what was coming to them. I had to think that God had a bigger plan for me and I had to try and sustain through the hard times on pure hope. Hope that I was going to live through high school, hope that I would get to go to college to escape this hell hole and hope that my life would someday be better than what I had endured for the first 20% of my life.

Chapter Thirty-One

*I had two people at school
who really believed in my future...*

After the fight, Benny kicked Bernard out. This was exactly what Mama wanted. He went to live with her, not caring about school, and Travie and I were once again left to fend for ourselves while Benny smoked his life and our rent away. The other bad thing was that he started dating Sharon again. I dreamed that he would come home with Renee', but that was just a dream. She was never coming back. We knew that it was only a matter of time that we were going to have to move back to LA, because Sharon was there and the eviction notice was posted on the door.

School was back in session and football was going great. I was a starter and Coach Johnson said he was getting some calls from colleges with questions about me. My grades were improving and I had met this girl, Ina. She was a pretty young lady and very smart. I had never had a true girlfriend, so I tried to treat her like royalty, at least to the best of my ability. We did not get to spend much time together because we lived on opposite sides of town and I did not want her to see what situation I was living in. I tried to shelter her from my problems because I felt like it was not her burden to bear.

The day soon came when Benny told us we were moving to LA. Not a surprise. I knew this was coming and I had prepared Travie for the inevitable. The only thing that Travie did not know was what it was like being there with those girls and their mother. He would soon find out. I dreaded living with Sharon, but I had no choice as usual. I had my snake that Renee' had bought me and knew that she was going to make me get rid of it, but I took it anyway. As soon as we brought it in the house she exclaimed,

"Get that creature of the devil out of my house." This was almost an oxymoron to me. She had the nerve to call anything else a creature of the devil. I guess she must have had a hard time looking herself in the mirror; her exclamation was like the pot calling the kettle black. But once again it was her house, so I donated the snake to my science class, at least then I could still see it. This donation made me despise Sharon, so I refused to speak to her. I was a selective mute in her house.

Life there was hell as expected. Aretha now had three kids, and Sharmony was wilder than before, running the streets every night and sleeping all day. They had no idea what school was, nor did they care. The house was run by two crazy teenagers and a mother who gave into their every cry. My selective mutism worked fine, as Travie and I did what we had to do to survive. The day to day life there was bad, but I thought that eventually the same thing would happen like it did before. Until one day Benny and Sharon came home proclaiming that they had gotten married. Married! I could not believe my ears. How could he marry that person? What was going on? Wow! I was dumbfounded by the news. What was going to become of me and this new situation?

Chapter Thirty-Two

32

I knew that you had drive and ambition...

When I was not working at Jon Douglas, football was my main focus. I knew that if I excelled in football I would have the chance to go to college and leave the hell of South Central. I wanted to make something of myself and football was my driving force to do that. As my junior year started, Coach Johnson made sure I was on top of my studies. He talked about some test called the ACT. I had no idea what that was, but he told me the better I did on the test, the more opportunities I had to get into different schools. Coach Chapel was all about teaching me technique on the field. I had two people at school who really believed in my future and I did not want to disappoint them.

As letters started pouring in from colleges, Coach Johnson continued to encourage me in preparation for the ACT. I was not a good test taker and knew that a lot hinged on this test. The day the test came, I was clammy and nervous. I tried my best, which was all I could do. Coach Johnson told me not to worry and that if I needed to, I could go to a junior college (J.C.) or a small Division III (D-3) school. I knew this was not going to be an option for me. A J.C. was only going to keep me in the hood for longer and a D-3 would not give me the exposure I knew I could get from a D-1 school. I was that good or at least I thought I was. Ina encouraged me as well. She told me I could always take the test over again and that she would help me study. I did not want her to have to do that, so I just said "ok," knowing that that would never happen.

My football career was flourishing while my home life was horrible. I was working as hard as I could and Benny and Mama were still doing drugs. Mama was rarely around; she didn't even know I was playing football. Benny had never been to any of my games to this point, but I never expected him to come, because that would have meant that he would have had to take time away from his drugs to show me that he cared. They did not even know that I was planning to go to college. No one did. I kept that to myself because I knew that if they found out they would try to crush my dreams, like everything else.

When my test scores came, I was completely deflated. I had scored the lowest score in the whole school. I felt like an idiot and determined, maybe I should go to a J.C., or even worse, maybe I was just not cut out to be a college student. No one in my family had graduated from high school, so maybe that was it for me. Maybe I was meant to work for Jon Douglas in an entry level position for my whole life. Maybe that could lead to a higher position over time. Maybe I just wasn't college material. But Coach Chapel had words of encouragement... Proposition 48. That sounded like an airplane, but I was ready to hear what it was, as long as it ended with me going to college and leaving South Central forever.

He explained that it was for students like me who possessed a large amount of talent and schools wanted them to play for the team. I would have to go to the school for a year, with financial aid, study hard and prove myself, and then if everything worked out I would earn a scholarship. I did not know what financial aid was nor did I know if I was cut out to be in college without a scholarship. I thought hard about just giving up on the college dream and just focus on Jon Douglas, but Coach Chapel continued to encourage me. With the help of Coach Johnson and Ina I was going to work to study for the test again. Hopefully I would get the score I needed to go anywhere because I wanted a scholarship without Prop 48.

I spoke with Mr. Douglas about my dilemma, and he told me that anything worth having is worth fighting for. He went on to say that if getting into college was easy everyone would do it. The most surprising thing was that he told me a story of a boy who had a slightly impoverished beginning but knew the power of a good education. Mr. Douglas inspired me and encouraged me with his words of wisdom, telling me that he was there to help me as he always had been. I was very confused by that statement. I asked him what he meant. Mr. Douglas replied.

"Eboni I know that was you who pumped my gas many years ago. I recognized your face as soon as I saw you at Jefferson. Though I did not know we would meet like this, I knew that you had drive and ambition, despite whatever circumstances you were presented with. You were a hard worker then and now that you are faced with your greatest obstacle, look at it and conquer it as you have always done." I was silenced by his words. I had never put two and two together, but as he spoke of the days that I pumped his gas, the pieces all came together. The black Mercedes he drove was the one driven by the man who had given me such large tips many times before. His words were my new fate. God had winked at me and I did not recognize the winks because I was so caught up in feeling bad for myself. If Mr. Douglas believed in me, I had to believe in myself.

I studied all the letters that came to me from schools all over the country: Notre Dame, UNLV, Kansas, Nebraska, San Jose State, Michigan, Wisconsin, Hawaii, Washington State and most importantly U.S.C... This was my dream school. Ever since I was young, stealing from the vending machines on campus, I wondered what it would be like to wear a Trojan on my chest...to sport the crimson and gold, to walk the campus of a private university, not as a wishful kid, but as a student. I had to go there. I knew that I needed a 700 on my ACT to get in any of these schools with a scholarship my freshmen year. After the second administration my dreams were shot. I scored a 470. The letters from the schools started slowly disappearing.

I fell into a depression and Ina and I grew apart. She had a much higher score than me and knew she had plenty of options for college. I was now stuck with only a few schools that still believed in me; luckily one of them was U.S.C. As my senior year came I was hoping that I could find a way to become a Trojan. I knew that I could visit five schools and U.S.C. was the first one on my list. My host was great. He took me to places in L.A. I had never seen though I had lived there for 17 years. I got to spend time with Keyshawn Johnson, who spoke extensively with me about being a Trojan, how he would take me under his wing and what I would have to do to succeed there both academically and athletically. I wanted to go there, period.

My next visit was to Kansas University, where an old teammate had gone. When I visited, I remembered how much I did not like him and knew that I could not be there with him for four years. The environment was not bad and the people were nice. I just knew it was not a good fit for me. After that I went to

Washington State. They had the number one defense in the country and being a defensive end, I was excited that I could potentially be a part of that system. They were on their way to a bowl game and the scenery was beautiful. I was not sure about the school because it was not very ethnically diverse and it seemed like it was far from everything. After W.S.U., I went to San Jose State, which I immediately knew I was not going to attend. It was just like home. We went to a nightclub the first night I was there and I could not believe that in Northern California there were Crips and Bloods. They actually got into a shootout in the club. It was like a flashback of home.

The last school I went to visit was Hawaii. I probably knew in the back of my head that I was not going there, but just to go visit Hawaii was an adventure. The coaches there thought I was not serious, so I had to convince them that I was. I just wanted to experience what I had seen on TV. I wanted to know if there were really beautiful places like that in the world. When I arrived, I had never seen anything like it. It was magnificent. Maybe I needed to reconsider going there. Their football program was not very good, but going to school in that environment would make up for a poor athletic program. It was a little too isolated for me, but I would be far from home and no one would ever bother me there.

After long contemplation I narrowed it down to U.S.C., W.S.U. and Hawaii. Hawaii encouraged me to take the ACT again. I knew that was not going to be an option. U.S.C. wanted me to go to a J.C. for a year and guaranteed me a scholarship pending grades and W.S.U. told me I could be a Prop 48 for a year. This was the hardest decision I had to make and my parents did not know anything about it. My brothers had not gone through this before, so I turned to the three men who had gotten me this far: Coach Johnson, Coach Chapel and Mr. Douglas. They all encouraged me, but did not give me a concrete answer. I thought that if they told me what to do, I could not make the wrong decision. I thought long and hard about it and determined that if I stayed in Southern California I still had my parents and their problems to deal with. They were never going to leave me alone. As much as I longed to go to U.S.C., I knew I had to get away from the madness. I decided to sign with W.S.U. and believe that this was the right decision for me and for my future away from drugs, gangs, my family, and the black cloud that had loomed over me for so many years.

Chapter Thirty-Three

"Do you think you are smart enough to hang with the big boys?"

After making my decision, I knew I was going to have to let the family know. To this point they did not know that I had been thinking about college, visiting colleges or even had the ability to earn a scholarship. This was my opportunity to leave the 'hood and never return. I knew that as soon as I step foot on the plane to Washington I would never look back. I was determined to make my life worth something, despite all the obstacles I had faced (and overcome) to this point.

After signing my letter of intent, which was a huge deal for me and the rest of the Jefferson community, I went home and waited for Benny. I had put a call in to Mama, but I expected she would not return my call for many days. I knew by then she would have heard through the grapevine of family and her crackhead friends. When Benny did come home it was late, but I knew I had

to tell him. As he entered, I hoped he was not high. But he was. He looked at me with a nasty look and said,
"What the hell are you waiting for and why are you looking at me?" I quickly let him know that I had important news for him. "What? You didn't go get some girl pregnant did you?" He responded in a nasty tone, which made me very angry. Here I was about to drop the biggest news of my life and he thought it was something about a girl and pregnancy.
"No," I snapped back. "I was in the paper today; I signed with Washington State today. I'm going to college!" Benny hesitated and stumbled to a chair. He stared at me as if I was a creature from outer space. I did not know what to make of his silence. Was he mad?... Happy?... Excited?... Disappointed?... Jealous?... I wanted him to say something, anything. After a few minutes he proclaimed,
"You think you have what it takes to make it in college without your family? Do you think you are smart enough to hang with the big boys?"
"Yes," I confidently replied. As a tear rolled down his cheek, he said,
"Then I'm glad for you son." He said nothing else, rose out of the chair, and quietly walked to his bedroom.

Benny's reaction was one I did not expect. I think deep down inside he knew that I was never coming back and was going to live life without being dependent on anyone else. He and I had had our ups and downs, but I think Benny understood why I had to go and he was not going to stop me, like the rest of the family. I knew that Mama's reaction was going to be different and that I was going to have to strategically work to get her to understand my decision. I hoped that she would not hear from someone else, but my wish did not come true.

There were no congratulations when I picked up the phone

and heard Mama's voice on the other end.
"You think you smart? You think you better than us? You think you can just up and leave and go to Washington without MY permission? Who the hell do you think you are? You need me, I am your mother and you are not going anywhere. You are as ungrateful as they get. And you think you can leave and mess with my money?" I just sat there, because I never had to get permission for anything. She was never around to give permission. I had done my own thing and made my own decisions since I was 6; now she wanted to lay down the law. It was in one ear and out the other. What was I supposed to say? Did she think I was going to engage in an argument with her? I was not even going to waste my breath.

As Mama ranted on the phone for more than an hour, all I could think of was leaving. I knew it was coming soon and I was going to be out of this hell of a life. I was going to miss Bernard with all my heart, as he was the only constant in my life. He was my sounding board and my guidance, but I had to go. Maybe he could come with me. I decided that I would talk to him about that, so he could escape the madness and we could continue to support each other and help each other. Maybe he could even try and get into school. The conversation with Mama abruptly ended with her saying,
"If you leave I will never talk to you, you unappreciative bastard." And then she hung up. The long tone that I heard was ironic, it was like a church bell, and I knew this was God letting me know it was ok.

The next day I spoke with Bernard about coming to W.S.U. with me. Though he appreciated the idea, he told me he had a couple pending cases, that would not let him leave and that he thought it would be good for me to be away from everyone, to be on my own and stand on my own two feet. I was disappointed, but knew that I still had to chase my dreams and do things my way. As graduation came close and closer I was in constant contact with my recruiting coach. I asked him if I could come up the day after graduation. I was ready to get the hell out as soon as possible and could not wait until August. I always thought my life would lead me to an early grave. In the back of my mind I thought that I would never make it to W.S.U. That I would die at the hands of some gun toting banger. That's why I wanted to get out, A.S.A.P. There was a shining light at the end of the tunnel and I was moving towards it at 100 mph, with nothing in my way.

The day I graduated was just another day to me. Everyone (Mama, Benny, Bernard and Peanut) attended, but I would have preferred if just Bernard showed up. Mama acted a plumb fool, whooping and hollering as if she had no control over herself. I just wanted to hide. Of my 10 tickets, that left me with 6 tickets, so I gave one to Jon Douglas, one to Coach Chapel and the other three to Ryan (a girl I had been dating since Ina and I went our separate ways.) As I walked the stage I looked at Mr. Douglas who stood and clapped, and knew that he had helped me make it across that stage that day. I hugged Coach Johnson as I walked down the stairs and took a picture with Coach Chapel. Afterwards, Bernard embraced me with a big smile on his face and told me he was proud of me. I knew that I was not going to have these people around anymore, but I was going to have to continue to build on what they had taught me. Though they said they would always be there for me, I knew it was only a matter of time before we lost touch, like everyone else and I would be alone as usual. As I worked my last summer at Jon Douglas, he gave me college pointers each day and encouraged me to seek out help all the time. I was blessed to have him, but soon I would be on my way to Pullman, Washington to start my own journey, make my own rules and create a future I knew I could have.

DESTINY

What controls your destiny?
What determines your fate?
Though you live in a society of hate,
It ain't too late to break free.
The evil that exists in this universe is a curse,
But what's worse, if you let it get you down your last ride might be in a hearse.
The vision is there.
You just have to let it guide you to your dreams.
Help you be what you want to be, so that you may Ride your streams.
God didn't place you here to be the victim of the gun,
Always on the run;
He placed you here to have fun, and share the wisdom
You've learned with your sons.
So that the cycle ends.
Now it depends on you
Do you want to end this tragedy that young black men
Are going through?
I do.
That's why I'm trying to make our gray skies blue,
I want this cycle to die.
So that my people have every opportunity to fly.
Fly to the endless land untouched by the evils of man.
Now I hope you understand
That I mean what I say,
This cycle ends today.
Walk with me and I'll show you the way,
The way to the life you can't see,
So that you can grasp your destiny.
Now the torch has been lit
And to make sure you never forget.
This is branded in your heart
Like a work of art
Now it's your turn to share the light,
So that your seeds can do what's right.
I've done my deed,
Now it's up to you to succeed.

Chapter Thirty-Four

34

I felt like I was in academic heaven.

After months of calls and begging to come early, my recruiting coach told me that I could get on the plane August 17. I could not smile harder. I felt as though a large weight had been lifted off my back by my two angels. I was about to escape the drugs, gangs, shootings, deaths and poverty that had consumed me my entire life. I prayed every night that I would make it to that day. I knew that Murphy's Law said now that my dream was coming true something bad was going to happen to me. Day-by-day I crossed off the days on the calendar and knew that it was closer cross-by-cross.

When August 16th came, I packed my bag and prepared myself for my adventure. I did not have much to pack, so my duffle bag was light. I went by Isaac's to see him one last time, as he was off to school on a football scholarship as well. I hoped that we would stay in contact, but realistically I knew we would probably never see each other again. I thought about visiting Ina or Ryan, but knew that they were insignificant in my life from that day forward. I returned home to count the hours until the cab came to take me to L.A.X. I was too excited to sleep, so I just sat there dreaming about college.

The next morning, I watched out the window for the cab. When the cab arrived, I grabbed my bag and headed out the door. As I approached the cab, Benny, Bernard, Travie, Mama, Peanut, Sharon and Sharmony came from behind the house. This was unexpected, as I knew they did not care that I was leaving. The goodbyes were short, no tears. Just a few, "have a nice time," or "keep in touch." I did not hug anyone but Bernard. He was the one I would long to see and talk to. As we embraced he whispered,

"Make me proud again. You are doing what I always wanted to do, but never had the courage to do. I love you with all my heart, remember that." A tear came to my eye as I sat in the cab. As we drove away, the family walked back towards the house. I watched Bernard as he stood alone on the curb. He watched the cab drive down the street. I could see he looked sad, but I knew that I had to make him proud and do what I set out to do, make something of myself.

☙ • ❧

After a nervous flight, I arrived at the airport to get a warm greeting from my coaches and other recruits. I was free. I had control over my life and nothing was going to stop me. They quickly gave us an itinerary of the events for the next few weeks. They told us that all Prop 48 students had to take tests for placement. This immediately made me nervous. More tests, I hated tests and knew I was not going to do well. I did not want them to send me home before I even got started, so I asked if there was anything that I had to study. They told me not to worry and that I would be fine. That did not reduce my anxiety.

After the test, they revealed my score, indicating that I was going to stay and W.S.U. I felt like another weight was lifted and I was back on my mission. I knew that I was going to have to pick classes and decide what I was going to major in. I did not know what my boss at Jon Douglas had majored in, but Business Administration sounded like something important so I picked that as my major, in hopes to land a position with Jon Douglas in one of his offices. I anticipated that I would not have to do much math with this major, but I didn't care... I was finally in college. I had fulfilled my dream. Now I had new dreams to accomplish: find my way around campus, learn how to study, earn a scholarship and graduate.

The first week was dedicated to freshmen. We had different activities to participate in, campus tours and dorm events. These were good for me as I got to know my roommate, Nyin, a little better as well as get situated with my surroundings. Being a Prop 48 I could not practice, but I wanted to get to know the team, the plays, and the system. So I attended practices, watching and helping out when possible, to get all the knowledge I could. I wanted to know at the end of the day I did everything I could to be successful. I knew everyone back at home was routing on my failure and I had to prove them wrong. I had overcome every other obstacle and this was no challenge, but an opportunity, so I knew I had no other option but to succeed.

Once school started, I thought that college was going to be extremely hard. I assumed that because my test scores were so low, I was not going to be able to keep up with my classmates. But to my surprise as long as I went to class it was not that bad.

I made the mistake early on of missing one class and I felt lost when I returned. I knew from then on that I had to attend or I was going to fail. Along with learning that attending class was critical, the professors and academic advisors gave me the tools I needed to be successful. They even offered me access to tutors. I felt like I was in academic heaven. If I would have had this help in elementary and high school I might have been a good student. I used my resources and even got help with a class which I had a rocky start in. I found out about office hours. These were prescheduled times I would go and see the Professor. With the professor's help and with the assistance of a tutor, I brought my F up to a C+ in two weeks. Things were looking good and I was starting to get the hang of college until the day when my world came to a screeching halt.

Chapter Thirty-Five

35

*I wanted to make him proud,
I was going to make him proud.*

As I entered my room after returning from class, in which I got a B on a test, there was a message from the stadium telling me to immediately come to my recruiting coach's office. It seemed urgent and I wondered what I had done wrong. As I walked towards the shuttle stop I contemplated in my head what was so urgent. Did they mess up on my test scores and I really was not supposed to be there? Were they kicking me out? Were they going to tell me that they were not going to be able to give me a scholarship? Was my financial aid not coming through? I wished the shuttle would move faster, I needed to know.

Once I got to the stadium, I quickly walked to his office. When I entered the office and knocked on the door, coach was waiting.
"You wanted to see me?" I asked hesitantly. Coach told me

to come in and have a seat. As I entered his office I could see the look on his face meant that whatever he had to tell me was not good.
"What is it coach?"
"Eboni I do not know how to tell you this..." He paused. With his hesitation, I spit out,
"Just tell me."
"Your brother was shot and killed last night."
I had just heard the words that I had feared my entire life. I burst into hysterical tears and fell against the wall. I could not control myself. I couldn't stop crying. I did not even know which brother. I almost immediately knew in my heart it was Bernard because Peanut remained in jail and Travie was just too young to be a victim of violence, but maybe I was wrong.
"Who?" I cried out
"Bernard" Coach said quietly. I began to shake with anger and distress. As Coach tried to comfort me all I could do was cry in the corner of his office like a baby. I could still feel Bernard's embrace from a month earlier. I could still hear his voice in my ear when I left. I wanted to make him proud, I was going to make him proud. How could I if he was no longer here? This had to be a bad dream. I wanted to pinch myself and wake up. I was numb all over and had never felt that way before. I wanted to escape, I wanted to leave, and I wanted to know who did this to my brother. He was all I had. Why? Why were all the ones who protected me taken' from me? First Winter, then grandma, now Bernard. It is unfair and impossible to cope. He was supposed to come up to W.S.U. with me after his court issues got settled. We were going to be together. Anyone but him... why?

As I tried to make sense of the information Coach told me that they would pay for me to go home for the funeral. I could not respond. All I wanted to do was hide. As I gained my composure and the tears slowed down, I stood up.
"I'm going to my room." I said softly.

"Do you want to call your father?" Coach asked sympathetically.

"Yes." I responded. Though I did not want to talk to anyone, I needed confirmation. I needed to hear it from Benny to believe it. As he picked up the phone, I knew this was a nightmare; it had to be. When Benny answered, Coach put him on speaker phone. As tears rolled down my face I asked,

"Is it true, Dad?" This was the first time I had ever called Benny Dad.

"Yes." He responded softly. I fell back to the floor sobbing with pain. He continued.

"He was in a car with a young lady at about three o'clock this morning. As he was trying to start the car when two guys approached the passenger side and started shooting out of control. The girl was shot in the face and your brother was shot twice in the head and four times in the body. The coroner said he died instantly and did not feel any pain." I started bawling uncontrollably again. All I could see was Bernard slumped over the steering wheel of his car, with the horn blowing. Benny did not mention that, but that is what I envisioned. It was like a still frame from a movie, stuck in my head. Benny continued.

"Your Mom got a call and the young lady's sister came to get her to identify the body. She was very inconsiderate and stopped at Taco Bell before taking her to the scene. But your mother did identify him and his car. They do not know who did it and have no leads from what they tell us. I'm sorry Tay." I wanted pure vengeance. I wanted to rip the hearts out of the chests of the guys who did this to Bernard. I could not believe what was happening or what I heard. It was wrong on so many different levels. I felt the rage climb higher and higher. It was consuming me. I was mad, hurt and upset.

"Son when do you want to come home? Your Coach said they will pay for you to come home."

"I'm not coming." I said distinctly.

"I can't, I need to be alone. I will talk to you later." I stood up and walked out of the office. I knew if I went home two things were going to happen. I was going to do something stupid especially seeing Bernard lying in the casket and I was not going to return to W.S.U. So I knew it would be best for me to stay in Pullman and mourn alone in silence. This was the best way I knew how. This was going to be the only way I could cope.

As I walked back to the dorm, my head hung low. I did not want to see anyone or anyone to see me. It slowly started to rain. I continued to walk. It was like God was shedding tears with me. I thought about all the times Bernard and I shared all the things we talked about, all the new things he taught me and the last embrace we had. I could hear his voice in my ear. The word kept repeating over and over like a broken record: "Make me proud again. You are doing what I always wanted to do, but never had the courage to do, I love you with all my heart, remember that." It was like he knew. I never thought that was going to be the last time I saw him. The last time I embraced him, the last time we would look each other in the eye. I could not hold back my tears, but the rain drowned them out. I felt like walking forever. I could have walked forever, or at least until this horrible nightmare ended.

It felt like an eternity before I got back to the dorm. I was so focused on my thoughts, that my steps meant nothing. When I arrived to my room, I shut the door and started weeping again. The rage took over again. I could kill whoever did this to him. I will kill them. I will find them and kill them. An eye for an eye, especially when it is my brother. I was going to make some calls. I was going to find out who did this and they will wish they never had. They will want to turn back the hands of time. They will get theirs if I had anything to do with it. As the resentment and thoughts of retribution filled my head, I soon fell asleep.

BERNARD

I can't begin to explain how much I miss you;
You are a part of me and understand what we've been through
You're my blood
And to see you gone causes rainstorms and floods.
The emptiness I felt when I was told you'll never grow old
Destroyed a part of me, as I lay out in the cold.
You fell victim to the hood, how could it be
I will never again hear your voice, your face I will never again see?
I thought we'd share old memories together,
Failed by the ills of the 'hood, which destroyed our forever.
I still can't believe that God took you away
I knew we had to die one day, but Lord why today?
I guess it was bound to happen
Living in the 'hood, every night somebody start capping.
See your luck ran out bro' and those six bullets turned you blue.
Not you,
As these tear drops flood my face.
I ponder and wonder who placed us in this cruel place.
They took your life from me,
Added you as another statistic, and threw your memories to sea.
Never looking back,
To them your worth is nothing and it's because you're black.
Yet to me you're everything.
You mean the world to me and to think of you is exciting.
Only time will tell when I see you at the cross roads,
The day of grace that will lift this heavy load
I moan for you.

Chapter Thirty-Six

36

I felt like it should have been me.

As I slept, I dreamt of the night Benny described. I could see Bernard clear as day. I could feel the heat from his body and the blood from his chest run down my hands. I could see the faces of the bystanders, the only thing I could never make out were the faces of the shooters. They were like blank canvases. As I would reach out to grab them, I would wake up in a cold sweat. The dream replayed all night. I finally decided not to sleep. I got up and decided to call Mama. Though I knew it was going to have drama attached, I felt it was the right thing to do.

Mama explained that she was taking it hard. Who wouldn't take the loss of a child hard? She told me that she was screaming frantically when she saw him; she said she became paralyzed and fell to the ground. She told me she did not believe it either and while on the scene she went up to touch his face: his body was still warm, but she stated he looked peaceful, like he was sleeping. She told him that she loved him, that we all loved him, and then she sang to him. She said this was the only way she could rationalize the fact that he was really gone. She knew that he was in a better place and that Grandma would take care of him and that he could play with Winter. This made me cry. I knew this was hard for Mama, but I could not imagine what she was feeling. I knew what I was feeling, but for the first time in my life I honestly felt bad for her. I talked to Mama for a long time. We reminisced about Bernard and the "good times" if that was what you called them. Before I knew it, the sun had come out.

I called Benny later that day. He was very quiet. Knowing Benny the way I did I knew he was struggling, but he was an internalizer. He never really expressed his feelings well and kept to himself. He, like me, did better when he mourned alone. He wanted to know if I was alright. I wasn't, but I told him I was. He asked again if I wanted to come down, but I knew I couldn't. I felt like a large piece of me was missing and I could not do anything to get it back. Bernard and I, more than anyone, shared a lot of ups and downs and time together. I would have died for him if given the chance and sometimes I felt like it should have been me. If I could give my life for one more hug, conversation, workout, dinner or just a moment with him I would. We had a bond no one else could, or would, understand and I knew I had to keep my promise to him and make him proud.

Peanut, being locked up could only do so much to support the family emotionally. He wanted vengeance just like me, and because of his location and previous record he was much more likely to act on his feelings. He would kill and show no remorse. The service providers at the facility he was housed at offered him counseling and support to cope with the grief and hopefully make it so he would not lash out. He was also offered a chance to go to the funeral, but he denied it just like he denied the services the jail offered to provide him. He mourned silently and could not wait to get out to avenge Bernard's death. Travie was the only brother who went to the funeral. Though not as close as Bernard and I were, Travie started to hang out with Bernard more after I moved to W.S.U. He was the only brother he had around, so they started going out and spending time together. Travie told me that at the funeral when he approached the casket he could not stand to see him and fainted. He said that he was spiteful towards the people who killed Bernard and if he could he would make them pay.

My whole family was spiteful, angry, wanted to get revenge and everything else bad. But I knew I had to live on with my memories of Bernard and make him proud. I wanted to pick up the pieces of my broken heart and spirit, but it was the hardest thing I had ever had to do. For months after Bernard died I had the same dream night in and night out. In my dream, Bernard and I were at the movies together sharing a bucket of popcorn. As we sat there I told him that someone had told me that he was dead. He would look at me, laugh, and telling me,

"Who ever told you that lied. We will always be together whether near or far. I am your angel and you are my angel. Make me proud. You are doing what I always wanted to do, but never had the courage to do, I love you with all my heart, remember that." And every time after that part I would wake up with tears in my eyes. As the dreams slowly started to fade away, I had come to grips that Bernard was gone.

The last time I had that dream, I felt God had granted me those moments with Bernard to reaffirm our relationship, my personal dreams, and that he was my angel. I knew that whenever I thought of him he would always be flying above my shoulder... he could hear me, see me, and when needed comfort me just like when we were together on our own. I knew how much Bernard loved me and I hope he knew how much I loved him.

Chapter Thirty-Seven

37

I was on the right track and moving forward.

As I healed I started looking at life very different. I always felt sorry for myself and my situation and always wanted a quick escape. Many times I contemplated suicide, but not anymore. I was given a gift and an opportunity and God was going to allow me to use it to the best of my ability to get to where I knew I could get. I still had a lot of pain from his death and I felt like ever breath I was taking was a little shallower because he was no longer on Earth. But my focus had shifted. I needed to keep my promise to him and now I was worried about Travie because of the dangers he still faced in LA.

My studies had slipped while I mourned Bernard, so I needed two tutors: They were my life lines. Anna and Fumi helped me recover academically from the pain and I ended up passing the first semester. Soon thereafter Anna and I started dating. She was a decent looking girl with a fair complexion, curves in all the right places and long blondish-brown hair. She knew what I had gone through with Bernard and supported me through my ups and downs. At the end of the semester as everyone packed up to go home for the month we were off, I looked around and knew this was not a hard decision for me. I was not going home. This never had occurred to me before and I did not even think about the fact that the dorms were going to be closed as well as the cafeterias. What was I going to do?

Usually they have places for athletes to stay when they are in contest, but we were not going to a bowl game, so that option was out. I could not stay with the coaches, NCAA regulations; I had no money for a hotel for a month... could I sneak in and out of the dorm? Would housing make an exception for me? Then Anna asked me to join her and her family. She lived about an hour away, and I figure since I had no other option I would take her up on the offer.

After spending time with Anna and her family for the holidays I realized how much I missed out on as a kid. The joy that they spread and the happiness they exuded was like nothing I had ever seen. I realized that the joy of holidays was not about the gifts and the food, but the security of loved ones and being around those who cared. My joy and security had always been being away from my family. To Anna, family represented all that was good, while to me family represented negativity, drama, self pity and everything bad. What I was escaping everyone else was running to.

Upon returning for second semester my focus was on my studies, football and Anna. I kept to myself and maintained a low profile, as I knew I was going to earn my scholarship and play I started working out, studying film and plays. I attended all of the spring ball practices observing and becoming a scholar of the W.S.U. football game. Anna and Fumi continued to help me study and stay focused. I was on the right track and moving forward.

As for my family, I maintained contact with Travie and ensured he was alright. I started making plans to have him come to Washington over the summer so I could keep an eye on him and make sure he was not going to be another victim. Peanut was still locked up and, according to Travie, with Bernard's death, Mama and Benny were using more heavily than ever.

Chapter Thirty-Eight

*I was working my way
up the totem pole of success...*

As the summer approached, I made plans for Travie to come to Washington for the summer. I even arranged for him to work with the video guys to learn how to video tape our preseason camps. This was a good way for him to make a little money, stay out of trouble and see what college life was like. I wanted him to know that with hard work he too could go to college and get out of the 'hood.

Anna and I were doing fine and I felt like we had a solid relationship. To this point, I never had thought about marriage because I knew that I never wanted any woman to endure what I had endured with my family and I knew that if I had a wife, she might. I was also very content with being by myself. After Bernard's death I realized that those you love the most are taken from you too fast, so I never wanted to have that feeling about a woman. She would often bring up marriage and I would deflect to another topic. I did not want to hurt her feelings, but I knew I was not getting married. Over the summer Anna went home, but we talked daily and would see each other for long weekends at least two or three times a month. We talked about finding an apartment together, but I was not on board with the idea, but after multiple conversations and weighing out my options, we took that step.

My hesitation was that I did not want to feel like I was going to be in a situation like I was when I was a kid. I never again wanted to feel like someone had control over me, my living situation or my life. But knowing that my name was on the lease I had a sense of security. Just as we moved into our apartment I got word that I was going to officially receive my scholarship. I was ecstatic. I had achieved my first goal. Being on scholarship meant a check for my housing, books, and most importantly my education. It also meant that I was going to get to play football at a Division I University. As I signed my papers I could not hold back my smile. I wanted so bad to have someone take a picture so I could send it to Jeanie. Though I did not want to rub it in her face, it would have felt good to show the woman who said I was not ever going to be something, that I was working my way up the totem pole of success while she continued to live her life in hell.

During the summer I worked hard hitting the weights, developing key muscles groups, getting stronger and trying to learn the plays. Though I did not know what the thought process of the coaches were this year, in regards to me playing, I just wanted to be prepared for anything. During preseason camp, my asthma got the best of me when trying to make my time in the running tests, but I was determined to get beyond this obstacle. I wanted to prove to them I was committed. So after practice I ran and ran and ran. I wanted to open my lungs up and prepare them for two a day practices, long games and most importantly the running test the next year,

Travie stayed with me until mid-September when he had to return to California. I was sad to see him go, but I knew he would be back. As school started I got into my routine: class, lifting, film, practice, dinner, studying with Anna and then doing it all over again the next day. Early in the season I learned I was not going to get the opportunity to play, as they had one of the best defensive lines in the country, but I still wanted to show my worth. While on practice squad I was regularly beating starters off the snap, pass-rushing, knocking down passes, false sacking and loving it. I knew I was headed to big places if I kept on this pace. I felt good. Really good. It seemed as though all the pieces were falling in the right places and my life was on an upward trend.

As my life in Pullman continued to stay on the upward trend, things back in L.A. remained the same. Travie was longing to leave, Peanut was still locked up, and Mama and Benny were still heavily using. I felt bad, but knew that I had to continue focusing on me, as I always had. If I didn't, I would end up back in the same cycle that I wanted to avoid. So with this thought process I ignored the calls from Mama and rarely spoke to Benny. The only one I regularly spoke to was Travie, just to make sure he was doing alright. I felt as though I had to disown my family to get ahead, but I needed to rid myself of negativity to continue towards my next goal... playing football.

As my sophomore year came to a close. My life was excellent. I had a great girlfriend, my brother was coming back for the summer, my grades had dramatically improved and I was on my way as a starter, potentially all PAC-10 in my mind.

Chapter Thirty-Nine

39

*I was slightly hurt,
but could do nothing about it.*

Over the summer Anna went to Mexico on an exchange program, though we talked daily, things just weren't the same. She was spending a lot of time with a few natives and seemingly had forgotten about us as a pair. A couple of weeks prior to her return she called to say she had been in a car accident with a young man, was scraped up, had some bumps and bruises, but was going to be alright. Though concerned about her well being, I could not get the speculation out of my head about the circumstances surrounding this mysterious car accident with this so called friend.

Living with Travie was fine. He was growing up and I felt obligated to get him out of the ghetto. We talked extensively about him attending W.S.U., but I knew his grades would not allow him the opportunity and because he could not get a football scholarship, I was going to have to work magic to get him in. I was determined to help, but just needed to figure out how. I let him know that I was going to work on getting him in the school, and that he was going to have to work hard the remainder of his high school years to ensure that his acceptance was going to be the right decision for W.S.U. officials. Travie soon returned to school, keeping his promise of hard work and dedicated himself to try and do what he could to get into Washington State.

A few days before camp, Anna returned home. We had just signed a new lease and were ready to start our junior year. As soon as she came in the door, I could read in her eyes that things were not right. After a few hours of talking about her trip and all the things she did, it came out. The guy she was in the car accident with was the source of her cheating. Though thinking back, I was not surprised. During our conversations while she was gone, I could hear the difference in her voice. I was slightly hurt, but could do nothing about it. We determined that we would live our lease out and remain friends, though free to date other people. She almost wanted the best of both worlds, date here and there, but still have me waiting in the wings just in case things did not work out. I was not going to have it and knew that I was done with her. At every point in my life, no matter what bad things had happened to me, I never looked back and I was not going to make an exception especially not for a girl, particularly one who decided that she was going to cheat on me.

As far as football was concerned, this was going to be my year. As preseason camp approached, I was in my best physical condition ever. I was not winded running, I could bench press more than anyone on the team and I was in the top 3 on team in leg press and the team doctors told me that I had no more indications of asthma in my lungs. As we entered preseason camp, I was at the top of my game, rotating with last year's starters, taking snaps with the first team and letting everyone knew I was there to compete for my well-deserved starting position. Until that one play which changed my football career forever....

The day was a normal one, a hard Wednesday practice though we could feel that practice was nearing completion. I was lined up, ready to get a quick get off when the ball was snapped, I was quicker than ever pushing my opponent back, inching closer to our quarterback, Ryan Leaf. The next thing I knew we all heard a tremendous pop. It sounded like gun fire. Then another pop, a second shot. I knew it could not have been gun fire, but what was it? As soon as I had enough time to think, a split second had passed and I felt this intense, excruciating pain in my knee. I was face down in on the ground and could not move. All I could do was scream in pain. Trainers came running as silence filled the practice field. They gingerly turned my body over as I sat up. I could not feel anything but pain. Pain in my knee, pain in my leg, pain in my ankle, pain in my heart, pain in my head. I had never felt anything as physically painful.
I wanted to take my leg off and throw it because of the severe aching coming from my lower extremity.

As the trainers examined me, they asked for assistance from two of my teammates to carry me to an awaiting cart. They drove me back to the training facility where they moved me to a table and had the head trainer poke and prod at my knee and leg. Was it broken? Something pulled? A tare? I just wanted them to do three things: tell me what was wrong, give me pain medication and fix it. They wrapped it up with a bandage, placed a large bag of ice on top and under my knee and called the team physician to look at it. After further examination he determined that I had torn my meniscus, which I had never heard of. He explained it was a rubber like C-shaped disc that protects and cushions your knee. He went on to say that it helps distribute weight evenly throughout your knee and with the type of injury I had, he thought was going to need surgery, but they needed an x-ray to make the final decision.

"How long will I be out?" I asked the doctor, hoping that this was not a season ending injury. I needed to be on the field.

"Well depending on the severity of the tare, if it is moderate, 2-3 weeks after the surgery, if it is severe 4-6 weeks." I could live with that, hoping it was moderate and that I could be back on the field, before the middle of the season. Two days later I had signed my consent and I was ready for the meniscus to be fixed in order to get back to the grind. I did not tell Anna I was having surgery right away. I felt it was none of her business. The doctors indicated I would be staying overnight in the hospital and would need someone to drive me home, so I asked Fumi to drive me home.

After the surgery I woke up groggy, but my knee felt a little better. The post op staff was monitoring me and surprisingly Fumi was right there by my side. They reported that while conducting my surgery they found that my ACL was torn as well, but they did not fix it because they didn't have my consent. The doctor indicated that it was a slight tear and I could play with it, but might need to have it fixed after the season. They said the meniscus was fine and that I should be able to walk in 5 days with rehab and I could be back on the field in about three weeks. Things were great. As I rehabbed and started working my strength back up, Fumi was right there for each step of the process. Anna, though caring, was inconsistent with her support and showed little concern about my progress. Three weeks after my surgery I was back on the field running and though not in full pads, moving closer towards my starting spot again.

Chapter Forty

40

What do you mean amputate?

As the next weeks passed, I was healing and upon further consultation, I determined to have my ACL repaired. The doctors ensured me that I would be able to play before the end of the season. If not I would be great for my senior year. After the surgery, there was excessive bleeding from my wound. It would not stop bleeding. I was changing the dressing upwards of 30 times a day because it was bleeding through everything I put on it. Finally one evening I had Fumi drive me back to the hospital. They admitted me and started running tests. They could not figure out why I was bleeding out so heavily. After the second day of tests, the doctors revealed to me that if they could not find the source of why I was bleeding out, they were going to have to amputate my leg.

"WHAT" I yelled out. "What do you mean amputate? Is it that serious? I'm bleeding. You told me it's not an infection, how could this happen? What did you do wrong? Do I need to get a second opinion?" The doctor started to talk...

"Eboni we cannot find the source, we are waiting on the results from one last test, but if we cannot find the source, you will die. The only option is to amputate..." Blah, blah, blah... He continued to talk, but I did not hear a word he said. All I could think of was not having a leg. I came to W.S.U. for opportunities, to improve myself, not to lose a leg in a freak football accident. I needed to focus. I did not want to get angry, but needed to release my frustration. I knew they were professionals, but what was I going to do? Would I be in a wheelchair? Would I need a prosthetic leg? Would I have crutches? What would become of me? I would rather die than go through this.

After the doctor left, I looked at Fumi and said,
"They are not taking my leg. I will die before I let that happen." Fumi tried to calm me down asking me if I heard the rest of the things the doctor said. I told her that I had tuned him out. She said that the test they are waiting on will reveal if I had a staph infection and if it was a staph infection, they could treat it without amputating. I wanted to believe that they would find a staph infection, but knew that the black cloud was returning. Nothing good in my life ever lasted for long and why would this be any exception? I knew that this situation was going to be no different. My time at W.S.U. was winding down. I was going to have to end my education, learn life over again with one leg and try to pick up the pieces of my broken life again. I knew the road of positivity at W.S.U. would end, but I never imagined it would end like this.

It took longer than expected for the test results to come. I waited, focusing on the inevitable. A day before my test results came in the news had spread like wildfire around the team and athletic facilities. I had more visitors then I could imagine and frankly I just wanted to be alone. I knew they were there to give positive words and encouragement, but I wanted none of that. I just wanted the news and then time to figure out my next steps. The coaches even came as a group before they headed to Seattle for the Apple Cup. They told me they were going to win for me, which made me smile. As the day ended, I watch the game on T.V. going in and out of sleep, but really thinking about this process and how I was going to cope.

The next day as Fumi and I waited for the results, I knew that I was going to overcome this obstacle. I had gone through the stages of acceptance: denial, anger, bargaining, depression and now I was at acceptance. Ready to move forward, I had seen the dedication and support that Fumi gave me and though she was not my girlfriend, I knew that if I made it through this we should be a couple. When the doctor came in to report the result, I could feel my heart pounding out of my chest. I'm sure they could hear it.

"Eboni, I have good news and bad news, what would you like to hear first?" In my head I thought, what could be good about amputation.

"Good." I responded in a rude manner. This was no time to play kiddy games, but if that was what made the doctor happy, I would play along.

"We do not have to amputate." My heart dropped in joy. I was relieved, but knew there was still bad news coming. "We found a staph infection and with treatment you should be out of here in a few days. The bad news is I do not think you will be back on the field until at least the spring." I took a deep breath, I could handle that outcome. Though I wanted to play, I knew that

I had to heal and the end result of not playing the rest of the season was better than having my leg removed.

When I told Mama and Benny about my injury, besides wishing me luck through the healing process, I got little sympathy. On the other hand, Fumi was right there providing me with the mental and emotional support I needed. I knew she was the girl for me. To this point I had never felt this way about anyone and wanted her to know how much she meant to me. During the following weeks, we played video games, dominos, cards and just hung out. She was my road dog and I knew I could count on her in every way possible. Though feisty, I knew when it came down to it she would lay down her life for me, and I had never had that in a woman. Because of these facts, soon we became an official couple and started our journey together.

January 1st, as our team sat in the locker room of the Rose Bowl, I knew that I should have been suited up ready to run on the field with team. Instead of Coach Price giving the pregame motivational speech, he let me do it. I got to talk about overcoming obstacles as a team and finishing what we came to do. As we ran out onto the field among the over 100,000 people, I could not help but feel like my job as a leader on the team was just starting. I looked up in the stands as the fans cheered and realized this was my first time in California since I left and I had not even returned home or even let anyone know I was there. I was there with my new family and that was all that mattered.

Chapter Forty-One

41

I locked up and could not move

I knew my senior year was going to be the best year ever. I had worked with the university to get Travie in - he was going to work with the video crew as part of his work study for tuition. Fumi and I had moved in together and were tighter than ever and I was healed and ready to play. Though I wished I had gotten some snaps the previous year, I could smell it in the air. This was it. The other positive thing about my senior year was that over the past three years my grades had improved to the point that I thought about going to Graduate school to complete my 5th year, but I wanted to leave all my options open.

Peanut was about to get released and Mama had invited me to come home for his release party (like he was the next big rapper to drop an album). I had not officially been back to L.A. since I left for my freshmen year and something in my mind told me that if I went back I could handle it, as I had been there months before for the Rose Bowl. Travie was going and wanted me to attend before reporting to camp. It was all too fresh in my mind – Bernard's killing, Mama and Benny's lack of emotional support through my injuries and the previous "stuff" I had gone through – so I decided to let him make the trip and I remained focus on my goals… Playing football and graduation as it loomed closer than I had ever imagined.

Once preseason camp had started, I was the fastest, most conditioned player on the team. The strength coach, line coach and head coach were all singing my praises. They liked what I was doing, and I seemingly had made a full recovery from the meniscus, ACL, and staph issues. The two-a-days were going well until I went hard against my rival and felt a long stretch in my neck and back. I locked up and could not move. The trainers came over and were afraid to move me. An ambulance was called and I was carted off to the hospital. I did not know what my fate was but it could not be good. Here we go again.

~

As I lay in the hospital waiting for the doctors to return with the results of my MRI, CAT scan and x-rays, I looked at Fumi with worry in her face. They had me strapped down to the gurney for precautionary reasons, as I had lost feeling in my legs. If there was damage to my spinal cord, they wanted to ensure I did not move and potentially cause further damage. I knew, or at least hoped, I was not paralyzed, but wanted to know what the problem was. I could see Fumi's eyes water up as we talked about how I felt. I did not want her to worry and I did not want her to know I was worried. She was encouraging but I knew she was petrified.

Soon the doctors came in with the results of my tests. They all showed no permanent spinal cord damage, but that they wanted to keep me under 24 hour watch for the next few days to see how I progressed. They said that though there was no visible permanent damage, because of the swelling and other nerves around the spinal cord, that it was likely that I would not play football again. He continued on by saying that I could still lead an active life after I was fully healed but due to the heavy impact football, had it could permanently damage my spine leading to paralysis or worse.

I was done. My world was crushed. Though football was not everything to me, it had been my means to an end for the past seven years, and I had no idea what I was going to do now that my football career was over. I tried to stay positive, but knowing my history and my pinned up anger and energy, I was going to have to find a new outlet or I was bound to wind up like I was in elementary and junior high school... in trouble.

Chapter Forty-Two

42

I called Mama to let her know my plans.

As I started the acceptance process all over again with my spinal cord injury and not being able to play anymore (and never going to be able to play in the NFL), I was allowed to take a more active off-the-field role with the team. Being a psychology major (changed from business administration when I found out how much math there was associated with business), I got to work on team development and awareness through workshops, classes and interventions I provided to my teammates. I was very happy about this because it allowed me to stay active and remain part of the family that had embraced me for four years. This also allowed me to work on my psychology skills as I knew this would be an integral part of my field base experiences for graduation. Through this process I got to meet the parents of my teammates, one of whom taught me a method to keep my mind occupied.

Being a student athlete, we had the perks of per diem checks, book allocations and meals at training table, but I always seemed to need money. Coming from nothing, I had nothing. So I was thankful for those extra funds I could get from helping someone in the gym or selling a baseball card here or there. But when I learned from a parent of a teammate, that there was a fast, legal way to make money, I was all ears. She spoke to me and a few others, about allowing her to take any extra funds we had and investing it for us. Though I really did not understand the process I was open to the idea. I just needed to see what she was talking about. The deal was to show me she would take $100 of her own, make money and whatever she made in a month she would give to me. So I was in, I had nothing to lose and if it worked, she could teach me or I could just give her my money and let her pay me. The other players must not have trusted her because they all laughed thinking they needed their money and could not wait for her to "potentially" make additional funds. So they did not take her up on her offer.

One month later she handed me a check for $237.
"You mean to tell me from $100, you made $237 in a month?" I asked. Now I was not the best at math, but I knew the yield on that was 237%. I also knew that was way more than the annual 2.5% interest any bank was offering in a standard savings account.
"Yes, it was that easy." She responded confidently,
"Now I cannot guarantee that the money I make you will be the same percentage each month, but I can almost always guarantee you that you will make more than you give me. You can also let me know if you want your principal and interest each month or just the interest. If you choose to get just the interest, when you are ready to no longer work with me, let me know and I will take your principal money out and you will be fine. The other option you have is to not get anything and just let everything

accumulate. But the choice is yours." As I listened to what she said, I was in a win-win situation. I was going to make money from the money I was getting and I could determine how I wanted the payout. The best thing about this deal was that it was legal, or at least she said it was legal.
"How did you do this?" I asked. I needed to know. I wanted a bigger piece of the action.
"The stock market" She replied. It is easy. I watch the stocks to see what I can profit off of in short quick increments, and then I buy and sell accordingly. It's pretty easy if you want to learn sometime I can show you." She had me hook, line, and sinker. I was ready to learn and make money from the little money I had. But I wanted her to work with my money and just show me what she was doing.

After the season, I continued to work with her learning the stock market. Fumi and I were preparing for graduation, but as commencement neared, I still had a fear of poverty. I was making a few hundred dollars a month with stocks, but that was not going to be enough to live off of, I did not have any perspective work opportunities and I was still terrified of the looming possibility of going home to the 'hood, poverty and hell I remembered so well. I knew that no one in my family had graduated from college, but I did not know what a college degree meant. I had to figure out what I was going to do with my future.

In February, my spinal cord injury was almost healed and I was looking forward to graduation and an uncertain future. I started talking to Fumi about post graduation plans and she said that she had decided to attend graduate school and that I should go with her. I had never seriously thought about post graduate work especially because I was not the biggest fan of school, work, reading or writing papers. I had really struggled during my first year of college and I did not know if I wanted to go through the same process for another two years. Furthermore, I did not want to study psychology anymore because at the graduate level I feared more study related to clinical application, which seemed boring to me. I really needed additional guidance on what graduate school could do for me... Where was Coach Johnson when I needed him? Instead I turned to Coach Price.

Coach Price suggested that with my work with the team and previous interest in helping others I should look at a graduate degree in education. He said that my scholarship could potentially take me through the program if I complete it in a year and that he could look into seeing how I could take a regular role in working with the team on a graduate level. He suggested maybe in teambuilding, psychology and weight training. As he spoke my mind started going a thousand miles a minute. Maybe this opportunity would allow me to coach or get a Graduate Assistant position somewhere. I liked the idea, especially because I was not going to have to pay for the degree. I agreed with Coach Price, let Fumi know my plan, went to my counselor and started the application.

My future seemed brighter and brighter. I knew with a Master's degree I would be able to get a job, though I was not too sure about education because I could not see myself teaching. After I received my provisional acceptance letter to W.S.U. graduate school, I was six weeks away from graduation and I called Mama to let her know my plans. She sounded good and said that she wanted to attend graduation. This had never crossed my mind; I guess I just figured she would not be coming to Pullman because she was never at anything else, so why would she want to come now. I told Mama I would think about it, but really I did not want her there. I had kept my two lives separated for four years and did not want them to merge now. After talking with Fumi, she convinced me it was the right thing to do regardless of the past, so I invited her and Benny to attend graduation, which was now less than a month away.

Chapter Forty-Three

I did not know what she was going to say but I knew it was bad.

The months prior to graduation, I had never made so much money in a short amount of time. While working with the stock market, and the parent of my teammate, by the time graduation came I had made about $2000. This was great and allowed me to start saving in a bank, instead of in my pocket, pushed up in my shoe or on top of the refrigerator. I did not let Mama or Benny know about this because I knew that they would beg and expect me to send them what they felt like was their "fair share." I put some of the money that I made towards my graduation party and got ready for what I thought would be the biggest day of my life.

When graduation day arrived, I sat in the apartment and looked around me. The apartment was quiet as Fumi was with her family. This was my time... my time to reflect, to remember, to celebrate. Many moments in my life had been spent alone, in the darkness, not knowing where my next meal would come from, when I would see my family again, or if I was going to be alive the next evening to think again. I had completed what I set to do. As I sat and thought about Bernard, I wished he could have been there watching and smiling as he did at my high school graduation four years earlier. He was the only one from my family who I cared about attending my high school graduation and I longed to have him be the only one to see me walk the stage and accept my college diploma. I needed him there. I wanted him there. Four years earlier he made me promise to do what he never had the courage to do and to make him proud. I hoped that as an angel he was proud. I hoped that he and Grandma would be clapping the hardest and cheering the loudest in heaven.

My robe hung on the door neatly pressed and my cap lay on the table. I never thought that I would make it to college let alone graduate and now go on to pursue graduate work. As I thought about how far I had come the doorbell rang. It was Travie, Mama, and Peanut. They were ready to celebrate my accomplishments. I grabbed my robe and headed for the door. This was the start of something new, something I had never experienced. I was about to receive my diploma…a piece of paper that symbolized blood, sweat, tears, hard work, knowledge acquisition and most importantly, pure determination.

As I heard my name called, Eboni Kentay Wilson, I humbly walked the stage. I received my diploma and stopped. It seemed like an eternity, but for that split second Bernard stood there and looked at me with the same smile he had on his face the day I left for college.
"Congratulations, little brother. I'm more proud of you today then you will ever know." I smiled back and walked down the stairs gripping my diploma like a badge of honor… it was my medal of freedom, my permanent ticket out.

Later that afternoon, Fumi's family, Mama, Travie, Peanut and a host of our friends gathered to celebrate our accomplishments. We had our diploma's properly displayed with distinction on the table in the dining room along with other mementos we had obtained along our college journey: Kenta clothes from my frat and her sorority, certificates of honor, my letters from football, pictures, and just items to remind us how far we had come in four years. We had a ton of food, the best BBQ there was... you name it we had it: ribs, chicken, steak, brats, hamburgers, potato salad, greens, macaroni and cheese, spaghetti, cake, ice cream, enough food to feed an army. We went all out; it was not every day you graduated from college. The house was full of joy and nothing could change the mood. I got to talk a lot with Peanut, who said he was interested in going to college and wanted to change his life because he knew he did not want to be a statistic. He knew that California had the three strike rule and did not want to walk down that road, being that he already had two strikes against him.

As we talked and caught up on the past, Fumi urged me to come over and speak with her. She had the same look on her face as she did when the doctor was discussing amputation with me. I knew something was wrong. I excused myself for a minute and we went into the bedroom.

"I don't know how to tell you this..." She started. I did not know what she was going to say but I knew it was bad and I did not want to have any bad news on such a wonderful day.

"Your stuff is missing."

"Huh?" I replied. I had no idea what she was referring to and I knew that no one had robbed us, so I needed more clarification.

"All your stuff we had displayed in the dining room, except for your diploma is missing."

"What do you mean missing?"

"Someone took all your stuff. It's gone." As I went to the

dining room I noticed that the handsome display Fumi had put together was now partially gone. All her items were still there, but my items were gone. Who would commit such an awful act? As bad as it was all I could think of was Mama. The previous 22 years flashed through my head, but if it was her, why would she do that to me?

I searched for her everywhere I could think of in the apartment but could not find her. She was nowhere in the house, outside, on the front lawn or in the garage. Peanut remained where I had just left him moments ago, but Travie was gone, my car was gone, and my items were gone. I waited and waited and waited. Though I tried to take my mind off the potential fact that Mama had stolen from me again, as time went on the more my anger grew and my blood pressure rose. I was unable to enjoy my party, my guest or my new found status as a college graduate. All I could think about was that my preverbal "white-picket fence" life I had created in Pullman, through hard work and not looking back to South Central, had been merged with the ghetto fabulous 'hood mentality creed my mother was so proud to live by.

A few hours later Travie returned saying that he had taken Mama to the airport in Spokane, because she said she had a doctor's appointment. Without hesitation I grabbed him,
"You didn't think for one moment that Mama was up to something, abruptly having to leave my graduation party on a Saturday afternoon to fly back to LA, for a doctor's appointment?" Travie paused...
"No." He said with hesitation.
"All my stuff is gone! Mama stole my stuff and I bet she is on her way to try and get any amount of money she can to smoke. Those were my memories, she did nothing to help create them, and you aided her in not only stealing my things, my moment and

my day, but her habitual drug addiction." I let go of Travie and left the house. I should have known something like this was going to happen. It never fails. Mama, with her drama will do everything to be the center of attention, ruin a moment for me and supply her drug habit in any way possible. If it was left up to me, I never needed to see her again. I would be fine with that and I was pretty sure it probably would have not made that big of a difference to her.

PERSEVERANCE

I was born into a society that gave little hope,
A society where a lot of my kind wind up on dope.
Yet I persevered.
I was told I would never gain success,
Yet I defied the odds because I did my best,
I persevered.
When my troubles were at their best and my back was
Against the wall
I stood tall.
Yes, I persevered
I tried and I tried,
Never accepting defeat and holding onto my pride
My ambitions for success never laid to rest;
My goals set high, and my emotions full of zest.
You can't stop me; you'll never hold me back,
There's no way I'll let you break my stride; I will never
Veer off my tracks
You'll never stop this train.
Though you may dish out some pain and give me a little rain
But I'll be damned if you cloud my sunshine
The destiny is mine.
Your thrust of hate, won't determine my fate
I will persevere.
Head high, showing no fear
Liberation is the only light I see,
My guiding star, my destiny.
Through my long journey of poverty, which try to retain
I stay focused, full speed ahead, riding my train,
And I persevered.

Chapter Forty-Four

I was clueless as far as what I could do...

As the summer started I knew I wanted to try and push through as much of my Master's as I could before my scholarship ended. I doubled up on classes and started taking courses right away. If I was going to have a free year to work on the degree I might as well try and get as much done as possible, that way I did not have to worry too much about financial aid if I did not finish before the year was over. I also needed to prove to the graduate college that I was worth the place they had provisionally accepted me in. Basically they needed to see over the summer if I was really dedicated and committed to the work necessary to complete the graduate program. I was determined to once again prove my worth.

I had not spoken with Mama since the graduation party, nor was I interested in doing so anytime soon. Travie and I were not on the best of terms due to what had happened at my party and though Peanut had nothing to do with the situation, we really did not talk either. We were never really close so I did not have much to talk to him about. It was like my life was back to normal. After the drama Fumi and I became even closer. Though she was not in the exact same program as I, we had a few classes together which actually made studying fun. I had never enjoyed studying, but she made it pleasurable. In addition to graduate school, I started working with the team as one of their strength coaches.

The joy of this position was that not only did I get to continue my muscle development, but I got to develop my understanding of my body, health, nutrition and its connection to self. Being that I never had a family to provide for me, I never learned about the importance of eating right, exercise and how it plays a factor in mental and emotional stability. As my understanding of the body developed I linked my learning with psychology and started work with the team on psychological development as it plays a role in football, physical endurance and performance.

After summer term, I had fully been accepted into the program and knew what the next year of my future looked like. As I worked diligently on my Masters in Education, I worked just as hard with the team. I worked to ensure that I was going to be done within the year because my scholarship money was running short. As I neared the end of the program I had no idea what I was going to do. Though I knew that the promise of finding a job was very good, I did not know what, where, or how to make my first moves towards finding a job. I was clueless as far as what I could do with a Bachelors degree in psychology and a Masters in education. Through many sleepless nights, I thought about coaching, but I was not inspired by this idea; being a teacher was not an option because I did not have a teaching certificate and social service would be too close to my memories of childhood. I knew I did not want to relive those trials day in and day out.

Fumi and I had a great relationship. I even contemplated that she might be "the one," and I knew she still had a year left in her Masters program. I never fathomed leaving the area as I did not want to be too far from her, so I decided to get the advice of Coach Price again. He knew me better than most and seemed to have some good ideas of what would fit with my personality and dreams. Never could I have imagined the suggestion he made about my future...

Chapter Forty-Five

Was I smart enough? Determined enough? Patient enough?.

A PhD? What? I could not believe my ears when I heard him suggest that I work towards my terminal degree. I had never in a million years even dreamed of being "Dr. Wilson," but it sounded kinda catchy. As with many of the things I had experienced, I did not know how to go about applying, what I would study, how I would pay for it, but I did know that most people who are doctors go to school for many, many years, which I did not want to do. Coach Price suggested I speak with one of the financial counselor who coordinates things for some of the athletes as well as an athletic counselor who could better guide me through the process. I left his office stunned about the possibility. What would Fumi think? How long would it take? Was I cut out to work on a doctorate? Was I smart enough? Determined enough? Patient enough?

When I got home I told Fumi what Coach Price suggested. She was thrilled. She thought it was a fabulous idea. I shared my concerns and she was reassuring that I could do anything I put my mind to. She said I was the most inspiring person she knew and that a PhD would only enhance what other people saw in me, which I had yet to discover. I thought about what she said. Maybe she was right. For so long I had been broken of my inner confidence and told I couldn't or I wouldn't or I shouldn't, that I never realized that instead of feeding into the negative expectations others had for me; I should have used it as a motivator to prove them wrong. As I listened to Fumi and thought more and more about it, I realized that I had overcome so many obstacles and that the end of the journey had to be this degree. I would once and for all prove that I could, I would and I did.

The next day I visited the athletic advisor who told me that traditionally PhD students took four to five years to complete the whole program. In the back of my mind I did not think I had it in me. She did review my transcript and told me that they could use my Master's degree course if I wanted to look into a PhD in Education. Using those classes and attending summer school she indicated that I could finish the course work in a year and then start writing my dissertation. She said the timeframe after that would be up to me.

"So I could be done in a year?" I asked surprisingly.

"I have never, ever, ever seen anyone finish in less than three, so I doubt you can do it." As the words came out of her mouth, I took it for what it was... Yet another person doubting my ability to do what I wanted, how I wanted. My thoughts from the day before ran through my head and I knew her words would be my motivator to finish in less than two years. With those words playing over and over in my head, I had to figure out how I was going to pay for the program. I knew that I had the stock market money, but that was not enough to pay for school, and I knew I still had rent, utilities and food to pay for once my scholarship ran out. As I headed to the financial counselor all that was replaying in my head was, "Eboni K. Wilson, PhD." Wow that's crazy. Mama and the rest of the family are really going to trip on this.

The financial counselor introduced me to the FAFSA and other aide paperwork. He told me that after I got accepted to the program to fill them out, return them to him and then the federal government would work their magic. He said because of my background and family history I should have no problem qualifying for full payment. I took the FAFSA forms, left his office and headed home to tell Fumi I was going to apply and work on my PhD. I could not believe I was about to be a doctoral student. The possibilities would be endless. As I drove, I became giddy inside thinking about the journey I had traveled, all the bumps in the road and what Bernard was thinking.

Chapter Forty-Six

As we sat there, my body got hot, I broke into a strong sweat.

As I entered the program I was very confident in my ability to complete the necessary class work for the doctorate. I was not so sure in my ability to write the dissertation. I had no idea what it entailed, but I did know it was very long, hard and time consuming. As I thought about the time I had invested in myself and those who had confidence that I could complete this process, I recognized that Fumi had been there for me through thick and thin. I had personally thought about us being together for the long term, but never realized the impact she had on me until I had the chance to reflect on the past five years of my life. As I thought more and more about it I decided that Fumi had shown she had my back through the highs and lows and I decided to propose to her.

After shopping for the ring, I set the plan to "pop the question." I was nervous/ I had never loved anyone like I loved her and I had never had a woman in my life like her. She was a strong black woman, the one I had dreamed my mother would have been. As we sat there, my body got hot, I broke into a strong sweat. She did not notice. As she turned to look at the commotion of the waitresses and waiters singing "Happy Birthday" to someone at the next table, I got on one knee. I pulled out a three stone engagement ring and had it in my hand. When she looked down and saw me, she immediately started to cry. I explained that I had never had a woman in my life that treated me the way she had. She was not only my girlfriend, but my best friend. I continued on with an emotional soliloquy and then ultimately asked her to marry me. She enthusiastically accepted my offer. Now that I was going to have a wife, my thought process changed from me to us. Though we did not know when we were going to walk down the aisle, I had to plan for my future and my future family.

As I started working on my doctorate, I immediately decided that all the work I was going to complete for my courses, would be on the same topic as my dissertation. I knew what I had gone through as a child and I wanted to relate my dissertation to something similar. I decided to do an ethnographic inquiry on at risk African-American males and their vision of the future. As I worked through my classes, Fumi continued to support me. My relationship with Mama and Benny did not improve, but it did not get any worse. Travie was working on his classes, but not as diligently as I thought he should and Peanut was thinking about enrolling at W.S.U.

At the end of my first year I had completed my classes and Fumi had an internship. She was going to be done with her Masters in December and my goal was to be done with my

Doctorate at the same time. Putting myself under pressure, I started the long haul towards writing my dissertation chapters. There were days upon days where I did not see Fumi, as I locked myself in a room, listened to Erika Badu, spread my papers out and wrote. My interactions with the team slowed down tremendously as I was on a mission to do what everyone thought I could not do.

Most things in life came easy for me when I tried. School was never anything I tried at because it was boring and a waste of time. Leading me through the doctoral process shaped my thoughts to see that even when you try and work hard, things are not always easy. I was once told, "If it was easy everyone would have a terminal degree" and that quote was quite true. I had never worked so hard at anything, but my will to succeed overpowered the grueling work, time and frustration that accompanied the process. Using what the counselor had told me about what she had seen (how long it took other doctoral students) and what a classmate, who had been in the program a year before me had said about finishing before me (and the $100 bet that went along with it) as my motivation, I pushed through, defended my dissertation, proved all the naysayers wrong, and completed everything December 16th: a year and a half exactly to the day I started. I was a Doctor!!!

Chapter Forty-Seven

I returned home to let Fumi know what had transpired.

After completing my Doctorate I decided to take a break using the money I had earned in the stock market which was about $9000. Fumi took on a part time job, but for the most part we just relaxed and enjoyed each other's company. I continued to interact with the athletic program, branching out from just football and I started thinking about exactly what my next steps were going to be. After about five months I started applying for jobs in the Seattle area because I loved the environment and Fumi had family there. Simultaneously, she applied for jobs in teaching at the collegiate level.

As my resume's started going out and the phone started ringing for interviews, I really started contemplating working for Washington State Athletics. I started talking to the Associate Athletic Director about a permanent position as Life Skills

Director. It was projected to be a new position where I would work with athletes teaching them about the transition to college, working with the team psychologists and developing a core curriculum for student athletes over the course of their four to five years at W.S.U. As we negotiated to create the position I got a call from Upward Bound. They wanted to interview me for a Counselor position in Seattle.

So three days later I traveled the three hours to Seattle for the interview. I had never really participated in a formal interview, so I did not know what to expect. It was not as formal as I thought, sitting in the office with one man, who reviewed my resume and started asking a gamut of questions about my thoughts about outdoor development, personal growth and education. As the interview came to a close I felt good and I thought he was interested in me. He told me he would be in contact in a week or two to let me know if I had the position. Upon returning home, there was a message on the machine from W.S.U. athletics letting me know they had an offer for me. I felt like everything was falling into place.

The next day as I prepared to go to the stadium to speak with the Associate AD, Upward bound called offering me the position. The pay was good and they even offered to pay a portion of my moving expenses. They wanted me to start right as school was getting out, which was about three weeks away. I told them I would get back to them later that day because I wanted to see what W.S.U. had to offer. As I drove to the meeting, I could not help but smile. I was doing what I never thought I could. I was about to have a job, making good money and never would I have to return to the 'hood or live an impoverished life. My meeting with the Associate AD went as expected. They offered me the Life Skills Coordinator position, but wanted to pay me way less than I expected. Though many people would have jumped at the opportunity to make $40,000 a year (just $5000 less than my boss at Jon Douglas), I knew that being a black male with a PhD; I was worth more than that. Graciously declining the offer, I returned home to let Fumi know what had transpired. I called Upward Bound and accepted the position.

I knew fate was working with us because the next day Fumi was offered a position in Seattle at a local college. We were ready to make the move together. We wasted no time, packed up our stuff and decided to move that weekend. Ironically, that Friday W.S.U. came back with a higher offer, but it was too late. I was moving to Seattle to start my life as a productive member of society and working towards marriage. I had overcome every possible obstacle and from that day forward, I was going to work to make my life better and better through continued determination and hard work.

Chapter Forty-Eight

*We both knew that we
were meant to be together...*

We decided to live with Fumi's grandmother until things settled down with finances and the new jobs. I enjoyed working with the children; they made me laugh and kept me on my toes. I never would have imagined that working with youth would be so rewarding and fun. As I counseled them on different life problems and explored physical and mental challenges, I started to realize that working with children was my calling. There was nothing else for me. I wish that I would have known sooner. Fumi loved working at the college and flourished in her position to the point that they wanted to move her to a new, higher position. Things were perfect. Though we had not set a dat,e we knew that it was only a matter of time.

One day while working with a group of boys I noticed an older man watching us. My senses were heightened and I needed to know what he was doing. During a free play exercise I approached him, asking him if I could help him with something. "You are inspiring," he exclaimed. "I know this man in Chicago, who is looking for a man like you to come work in his school. Would you be interested?" I did not know what to say. Chicago? I had never thought about moving that far away. My life was going well. Who in their right mind would throw a monkey wrench into their finely tuned machine? What would Fumi do? How would this work? As the questions flowed through my mind, my mouth was on a different wave length.

"Sure I would be interested." I responded. What was I thinking? I had just started working for Upward Bound. In my mind, though I had all the looming questions, I knew it would not hurt anyone or anything to look. So he put me in contact with the Executive Director of a Charter High School in Chicago, Mr. Lang. He wanted me to interview with the organization for a teaching position which would possibly lead into an administrative position down the line.

Fumi was skeptical, but encouraging, knowing that she was moving up in position and had a good job. We both knew that we were meant to be together so it would work out for the best. As I flew to Chicago, I was nervous. What was this going to be like? I had never taught a high school class. I never liked school. Now I might be teaching in one. I just was so confused. Upon arrival, I got a tour of Chicago, the school and a brief introduction of the demographics and student make up of the school. I met with the interview team, which was much more formal than my interview with Upward Bound. I sat at the head of the table, while a team of people questioned me from a long list of interview questions they had prepared. I thought I handled myself well, but was unsure as I was sweating bullets. I knew that I still had to meet with Mr. Lang who I had been in contact with to coordinate the trip and interview.

After the committee was done talking to me, I sat in the room and waited. After ten minutes a large man entered the room. He was tall and possessed a distinct presence. He approached me with his hand out.

"Eboni?" He asked. I stood up.

"Yes." I replied.

"I'm Mr. Lang, nice to finally meet you." He shook my hand. His shake was strong and firm, but not too over powering. As he sat down he invited me to sit. We then chatted about this and that, never really talking about teaching, education or the position. After about a half hour he paused and looked at me.

"I want to hire you." Wow, I thought. That was not expected. I thought they would send me back home, give me a call, let me contemplate it. Never did I think this was going to happen. I hesitated to say anything.

"I know you live in Washington, I will help you find a place out here. I want you to start in a few weeks. The pay we can negotiate and you will have full benefits." This was an offer I could not refuse, but I did not want to seem over excited or needy. I knew I needed to talk with Fumi and see what we were going to do about her career.

"I need to speak with my fiancé and see how we will work this out. I am very interested; can I let you know tomorrow after I return home?" I asked.

"That would be fine, but I need to know, so I can put things in motion on my end. I like you Eboni and I think we will work well together. This is a great place to work and I think you have a lot to offer the population of students we serve. Call me tomorrow." I left the school, headed for the airport shocked. A job in Chicago. Chicago, I knew nothing about Chicago except Michael Jordan, Walter Payton and hot dogs. What was Fumi going to say? How were we going to work this out? I knew God had to have a plan, but what was it?

That night I sat with Fumi and we hashed out all the options.

We decided that I would move to Chicago, she would help me find a place and move and then after next year she would look for something in the area and move out. I couldn't help but feel like this decision was the best for me but not necessarily us. She was encouraging and promised that it would work out. I had to believe what she was saying because she had always been right before and our love had brought us through everything else.

The next day I called Mr. Lang and accepted the position. I could not believe it. I was moving half way across the country. This was really a new start. I called Mama, Benny and Travie to let them know my plans and they had nothing but good things to say. I had never heard Mama or Benny encourage me. This let me know that I had done the right thing. God was winking at me again and I had to embrace his wink. The next day, I started researching Chicago, finding places to live and preparing myself to resign from Upward Bound.

Chapter Forty-Nine

49

The biggest difference was the time.

Moving to Chicago was pure adventure. Fumi helped me pack my things and I arrived to find the place that Mr. Lang had recommended not very pleasant. It reminded me of L.A. So Fumi and I sought out somewhere the two of us knew we would be comfortable. It led us to a small community outside of Chicago in Indiana. It was a quiet nice neighborhood and not knowing much about the area, I felt like this was the place for us. The next few days Fumi helped me get settled and as she flew back to Seattle she had made plans to return in a few weeks.

That night I sat in the apartment and looked around me. It reminded me of when I was young, in the apartment Mama had left me in for so many months. The difference was that I had food, lights, central air and heat. This was my place and I was going to pay my bills on time to ensure I was never going to get evicted. Fumi called me letting me know that she had arrived safely. I felt emptiness in my stomach. I missed her and wanted her there with me. I had had her by my side for so many years, and without her I felt like a piece of me was missing. I fell asleep that night on the couch knowing I had a full weekend ahead of me as I had to go into work Monday.

~•~

Monday came and I arrived to work early. Mr. Lang greeted me, showed me my classroom and instructed me on the institute days I had to participate in. The next week I sat through meetings and daydreamed about life in Chicago, learning my way around, the city, and learning the differences between living in Washington and Illinois. The biggest difference was the time. I felt like every day went so fast because I was two hours ahead of Seattle. I spoke with Fumi every day; I longed to have her with me and could not wait for her return.

When school started things got better. My days were filled with lesson planning, grading, after school activities, and meeting with students to ensure they understood what I taught. I never wanted any of my students to feel like they could not come to me for help or to fail because I had not done everything in my power to help them pass. Mr. Lang saw my hard work and acknowledged what I was doing through a bonus and more responsibilities within the building. Things in Chicago were not that bad. The only downfall was that Fumi was not there to enjoy it with me.

The week finally came. Fumi was to fly out Friday to spend the weekend with me. I was ecstatic. The days flew by. I had not spoken with her in a while, due to the time difference and our extensive hours at work. Many times, by the time I sat down to call her, she was still at work and then when she could call me I was already asleep. When Thursday came I knew I only had one more day. I made it a point to stay up to accept her call because I needed her flight information and just wanted to hear her voice.

"Hello Baby, how are you? I can't wait to see you tomorrow." I answered when her call came through. There was silence on the other end. "Hello?" I questioned.

"Hi, Eboni." She responded coldly. She never called me Eboni unless something was wrong. What could it be? Tomorrow was going to be great. She did not sound excited. I waited.

"I hate to tell you this, but I can't make it tomorrow. The college is sending me on a retreat to Washington D.C. and it is mandatory, but I will be there in a week or two." My heart dropped. But what could I do? She was doing something for work and I had done what I had to for work. Though discouraged, I said it was fine and we agreed to talk that weekend.

The days passed and I did not speak with her. In my heart I knew we were growing apart, as long distance relationships were probably the hardest thing to maintain. I loved her, but knew that we were not on the same path anymore. A few weeks later she called and let me know that she had met someone else. She said that she wanted me to know before her feelings for this other man grew stronger. Though hurt, deep down inside I knew our break up was inevitable. She asked me if I wanted the ring back, I told her it was hers. She told me that it was never her intention to let this happen. I knew what she was saying was the truth, but I could not help but blame myself for leaving and not staying in Seattle with her at Upward Bound. I had to chase my dreams and in the process, I lost the best woman I ever had. After we hung up, I knew I would never hear her voice again. I sat in the living room, knowing this was my time to focus on me; I needed to get my thoughts, emotions, and life together. I knew I was not going to date for a while, learning that to be one with someone else you have to be one with yourself and I was not there yet. The next few months I focused on work, learning the stock market better, working out and maintaining myself mentally. I hoped this internal focus would lead to my betterment, and soon to my surprise it did.

Chapter Fifty

50

You were an example for me even though no one was an example for you.

As I continued to work at Longwood, I started to see that education was the career for me. Over the next year and half I immersed myself with teaching, education and working with the students. At the end of my second year I had moved from teacher to Dean to Assistant Director to Director. Though I did not have the day to day lesson planning and instructional contact with the kids, I continued to get to help them and problem solve their issues while helping teachers teach. Mr. Lang and I worked well together and had an understanding about how the building was run and how the students were going to achieve, both educationally and socially.

I had slowly started dating again, though I compared everyone to Fumi. There seemingly was not anyone out there who compared to her or anyone who deserved my time. Travie was almost done with school and decided that he was going to come visit me. I did not mind because he was my brother and it would be good for him to see what I did and how life after college really was. He made plans to fly out the next Thursday. I thought about bringing him to the school to meet Mr. Lang and see the kids. Though he had no desire to go into education, it would be nice for him to see what I did for a living.

When Travie arrived, I was happy to see him. He looked the same, just older, and though his appearance showed maturity, his jokes and clowning did not. He was the same silly Travie. While driving to the apartment Travie opened up to me.

"I want to thank you." He said.

"What for?" I replied wondering where he was going with his statement. Travie continued,

"For so long we lived a life of hopelessness. I thought that was how it was supposed to be and going to be forever. I never dreamed of anything else except for the life in the ghetto that I knew. But you changed that. You changed the course of our family by aspiring to do what everyone thought we could not do. You challenged yourself to go beyond what other's thought and what others said you could not do. You went to college, you got out. You were an example for me even though no one was an example for you. Now look at you, you are a PhD, have a good job, nice place and left behind the 'hood. Even more, I want to tell you that Mama and Benny are both clean now. They have turned their lives around. Benny left that women and is working and Mama is thinking about going to school to complete her GED, maybe even get and Associates degree. Peanut is even applying to W.S.U.; he wants to know if you can help him get in. You changed our family and our future forever." I paused, then responded,

"I guess I should say you're welcome, though you do not have to thank me. I was just doing what I had to do because I knew that I did not want to stay there forever. I'm glad that it motivated you and hopefully will motivate Peanut, Mama and everyone else. I'm happy that the future is different because of my decision. No one should have to live like we lived, nor should anyone have to settle for a life they do not want. I didn't."

There was silence. I looked at Travie who had tears in his eyes; I really had changed his life. As we rode in the car I was proud of Travie, Mama, Benny and Peanut. I did not know my life meant that much to them, but I was happy to hear the family was moving towards something more positive than drugs, gangs and the 'hood mentality. I never thought that my actions influenced or affected anyone but myself, but with this news I guess that I had made a difference. I was happy to hear Mama and Benny were clean. That was the greatest thing I could ever imagine. I just hoped that it was permanent. We drove the rest of the way in silence, there was not much more to say.

The next day I took Travie to Longwood. He loved seeing the kids and talking with the staff. He asked me if after he graduated I could get him a job. I told him I would look into it, but never thought he was serious as I knew he wanted to return to L.A. after he graduated. The rest of the weekend was spent shooting the breeze, joking around and reminiscing about old times. Travie was always a joker and knew exactly what to say and do to make me laugh. It was good to spend time with him; I had not laughed that hard in years. As the weekend came to a close, I was going to miss having him around, but I needed to remain focused on my career and my life. He returned to school and I returned to my life in Chicago, until I got the offer of a lifetime...

Chapter Fifty-One

The young man had never seen anything like that before.

About half way through the school year the phone rang with an offer I could not refuse: an Assistant Principal position in Chester, Pennsylvania at a high poverty, urban school struggling to make any type of academic advancement with multiple discipline problems. They needed two people to come in and turn the school around A.S.A.P., and Mr. Lang and myself were thought to be the two who could do it. Upon meeting the students in a large assembly format, Mr. Lang left the building telling me, the kids and staff were crazy and he was not going to be any part of it. The company then offered me the Principal position. Understanding the dynamics of the students, staff and low expectations, I was unsure if this was going to be the right career move for me without Mr. Lang. I could have easily just went back to Longwood and continued my work there in my comfort zone.

That evening I looked to the heavens and asked Bernard what he thought. I needed help. I asked God to give me a wink, a sign, that I should take this position. As I waited for some big miracle to hit me in my face, I turned on the TV. As the picture got clear the voice over said. "Tonight's movie special is 'Lean on Me.'" This was my sign. God was telling me that I had to go in and help the kids that others had forgotten. I had no other option, but to listen to my angel and God. So I accepted the position, leaving Longwood and moving to Pennsylvania.

When I arrived in Chester it was way worse than I could ever imagine. Teachers, students and staff were doing everything but teaching. I had my work cut out for me. I immediately started moving security guards around, making them responsible for student safety and I personally made rounds every period. Students were used to being out in the hall, cursing and fussing, not paying attention to the fact that they were in school to learn. They were not used to someone like me. I was a principal who was visible and not afraid of conflict resolution. One day a young man thought he was going to intimidate me by getting in my face and thought I was going to back down. There we were the two of us, face to face in the hall way. Though I was not going to initiate anything, I did know that if I had to defend myself I would. The young man had never seen anything like that before. He had obviously tried it with other adults and he ended up backing down. I knew I had to earn the respect of not only the students, but the staff, and being visible, firm, but fair, and exhibiting tough love was the only way I was going to do it.

As the word increased about what I was doing, the press got wind of me... The new Principal. I was heralded as the man who saved Chester. The principal of all principals. The Turn-Around King. They embraced me like I was the greatest things since sliced bread. I was on the cover of newspapers, news reporters interviewed me, and radio shows were calling left and right. I did not care about all the attention. I was there to do a job, help kids and ensure they had a better future because they were invested in their education. With all the attention came a lot of haters. I never knew what people meant when they say if you don't have haters you are not doing what you are supposed to be doing. I must have been doing something right, because I had a ton of them.

I figured many of the people there did not like me for one reason or another... maybe it was because I was bigger than most, muscular black guy who had a PhD, maybe it was because I took nothing from anyone, maybe it was because over time the students grew to respect me and actually started to go to class and work or maybe it was because I turned an adversarial staff around to work with me instead of against me or maybe it was because I held everyone, including myself, accountable for the education we were providing students. I don't know, but whatever it was someone was out to get me.

One day while doing my rounds, I made my usual stops: the cafeteria, the third floor, teacher's lounge, through the auditorium, up each flight of stairs and down the multiple hallways and corridors. Upon my return to the office I got a call from the dean's office stating there was a problem with a young lady being found in the auditorium. I inquired if they needed me, but got no response. I continued through the rest of my day, thinking nothing of it. Three weeks later my life was turned upside down. A firestorm had erupted. The young lady who was found in the auditorium during class time, had accused me of having sex with her. My world had come to a complete halt.

"WHAT? I did no such thing." I responded to the authorities and my boss while seated in my office.

"Dr. Wilson, we have video tape of you entering the auditorium during the time the young lady was there. We are going to have to take you in, you are being charged with indecent exposure and corruption of a minor." My world sank. Why? Why would she accuse me of such a horrible thing? This was going to ruin my life, my career, my dreams. As I was hand cuffed and marched out the front doors of the school I was humiliated and embarrassed. There was media everywhere. Camera flashed, reporters stuck their microphones in my face, parents watched in disgusted and students just gawked while the whispers ran through the crowd. I did not want to say anything, but I felt that my voice needed to be heard. My attorney's cautioned me not to respond and told me that they would handle everything.

I was released eight hours later, posting a $50,000 bond, and left the station without many people seeing me. I went home to contemplate my life, my future, why this was happening to me and what I was going to do. In my heart of hearts I knew that time would allow the truth to come out, but what was I going to do in the mean time? My reputation was at stake and everything I had worked for was about to be for nothing because a girl lied. Why? All I could ask was why? I looked towards the heavens and asked God to give me strength. I had overcome so many things in my life, but I needed strength to get through this situation. My phone was ringing off the hook. It was nothing more than people wanting the dirt, no one who really cared for me. Mama did not call, Benny was nowhere to be found. I was alone. Just me and my thoughts, it was like I was ten years old again.

The next few months were horrible. I was not allowed anywhere near the school, as I was put out on administrative leave. The organization which I was employed with seemed to believe me and was supporting me, but not as much as I needed. I soon sunk into a deep depression, questioning myself, my abilities and my goals in life. I could not understand how I could dedicate my life to kids and have this happen. My life around me started to crumble. I needed to isolate myself from the world and hide. I felt like I was a kid again. Most days I spent going to the gym trying to release stored up energy and waiting to hear from my attorney's about the next steps. I was really struggling mentally. I was there to help the kids and guide them to a better future, I had worked for them and this was the repayment I got. I always believed that you are supposed to be innocent until proven guilty, but I was guilty in the eyes of everyone in Chester and the police were going to have to prove me innocent.

As my emotions slipped away from me, I started to lose weight and stress about everything. My doctor warned me that my blood pressure was sky rocketing and that if I did not release the pinned up stress I was going to have a heart attack. I was put on a borage of medications, heart monitors and they encouraged me to continue working out, with a low sodium diet and lots of sleep. Who could sleep? I tried to steer my mind back to the positive, telling myself that everything happens for a reason, that God would give me strength. Bernard had a plan, Grandma was watching and Winter was holding my head up. That never helped. I wanted to leave. Though I knew I was innocent, I wanted to disappear because then it would go away. I needed to run and keep running until everyone I knew forgot all about Dr. Eboni Wilson.

Months had passed and my depression and health never improved. The noise about my arrest never really seemed to die down, as there was always some type of buzz about me, the school or the "pending charges and trial", until the day I got the phone call.
"Turn on the news Doc, turn on the news." The voice on the

other end exclaimed. I was not really sure who it was, but I did as they said. There it was live on TV, the girl was recanting with a local news reporter. She said that she knew she would get in trouble with her family if they found out she was not in class and thought by saying what she said she would not be in trouble. She said that she did not mean any harm to me and never thought it would turn into what it did or that I would get in so much trouble. She said that she did it because I was an adult and could handle things better than she could. She apologized and handed the reporter a letter with the same thing written down. I was dumbfounded.

I called my attorneys who had received the papers that the charges were officially dropped. I was relieved. I wanted to scream with excitement, jump for joy and announce to the whole world. Instead I sat there. I was sad that the young lady felt the way she did. I knew that there was a bigger lesson to learn from this. It was not about me, but about the students, the ones who felt like they could only escape if they lied on others. The ones who needed to learn that you do not have to hurt others to get ahead. The ones I entered education to help. I sat and reflected upon the events of the past two months and knew that my calling was to help those who do not have a way out see that there is always a way out. I, through my suffering, had grown stronger and now I had to teach others that strength as well.

.

MY SOUL CRIES

My soul cries because innocent children are losing their lives
I despise the demise that's been hidden, the lies, which are causing
The cries in these ghetto kids' eyes.
I notice the injustice that's causing a disservice in the quest to
Understand what our purpose really is
This system is holding us hostage because it continues
To damage our image
Now how did we manage to let the system take advantage of our
Voyage through life?
We continue to salvage our roots, giving up one by one, by selling
Our souls like prostitutes
Now we refute and dispute against those who try to bring us out of
The dark
Illiterate to the deliberate demise from the start
Why can't we articulate the immaculate essence of black?
Embrace it, because it's in a fragile state and bring it back
Our heritage has been lost for so long that we must salvage
What remains
We must break these psychological chains, so that we may

Duplicate, better yet, triplicate its delicate remains

Don't think for one second that our setbacks were an accident,

Because this manifestation that we are living in is deliberate

We are so far gone and don't know right from wrong, that you think

My words have no validity

You think by going against this standard and following

A new path is too risky

What a pity

Don't you see that the life that surrounds you is gritty

I'm just trying to smooth out your course a bit

I am truly trying to inspire you to embrace education, so that you

Don't quit

I know your world is turning and it's turning quick

But until you recognize this cycle, your world is going to

Make you sick

You'll die living this standard, just as you were trained

I just pray you recognize the disguised trap, so that you

Break the psychological chains

Chapter Fifty-Two

I wanted to help them overcome the urban obstacles...

Though I was able to return to Chester, I decided to ask the organization for a transfer. They realized the situation that I was presented with and backed my transfer. Due to all the problems, they pulled out of the contract they had with the school board a year early. Ironically when test scores returned it revealed the first increase in scores the school had had in over six years. I knew that if I would have continued there, my influence would have been monumental for the students and academic achievement, but the obstacles were too great to allow me to stay there.

I was placed in a consultative position where I was brought to struggling school districts to assess behavioral and academic data to develop strategic, targeted plans to address predetermined areas of need. I traveled to multiple schools across the Midwest and implemented plans to increase student achievement.

As much as I liked my job, I didn't love it. I long to be back in a permanent position in a school where I could develop long term relationships with students and their families to help shape their academic futures. I wanted to help them overcome the urban obstacles they faced to have futures brighter than they ever could imagine.

Around the same time I got the new position as a consultant, Travie was looking for a job. Newly graduated from college he asked me if I could try and get him a job at Longwood. Though I knew that Mr. Lang did not have any positions, I thought the least I could do was give him a call. So I did.

After a small talk Mr. Lang told me he had news for me.

"Eboni I heard CICS is looking for a Director of a new high school just down the street from the school here. I think you should apply." CICS was the organization which supervised Longwood; though they did not run it. I knew the position would allow me the chance to have my own school again and fulfill my desire to build relationships with students like I had at Longwood. I knew the demographics of the student population and that the school was slotted to open the following year and increase in size each year until it was at capacity. It was not a bad idea.

"Who do you think I should contact or how can I apply?" I asked.

"Call CICS, they will tell you." He responded. I thanked him and told him I would call him soon. I wanted to contact them to let them know I was interested. I was so encouraged by this news I forgot to ask about Travie.

I immediately called CICS and inquired. Luckily it was not too late and they set up an interview. I was nervous, but I knew I could lean on my previous skills as a Director and Principal as well as knowing the Chicago community as one of my strong points. I did not know as much about curriculum, but I was willing to learn. I could work with some people I knew to help me with those areas of weakness and surround myself with people I trusted, especially because it was going to be a new school. In my mind, a new school meant new staff, no history, and no baggage. I was energized about this potential opportunity and knew that I had the chance to shape lives again.

❦

The day came for the interview. I was not nervous, just relaxed and confident. I knew that this was going to be a good fit for me and that if I got the position I was going to be able to build the school from the ground up, with my vision, my expectations and my leadership. The interview was as formal as they get. I sat at a huge table in an office building downtown Chicago with a panel of people asking question after question. There was a writing portion and a second panel interview. The whole process took about three hours. When I was done the CEO came out and thanked me. She let me know that they would be contacting me by the end of the week to let me know if I moved onto the next round. The next round? Wow. I thanked her and hoped for the best.

As I drove home I could not help but think about all the things I would do if I got the job. I wanted the school to be a model for other schools and stress academics and post secondary options. When I got home I called Mr. Lang. I told him about the interview, but it was like he already knew. He told me he heard I did a great job and that I had nothing to worry about. I did remember to ask about Travie, and he told me he thought he did have something. He told me to have Travie contact him.
That news allowed me to forget about the interview for a split second until the other line beeped.

It was the CEO. They wanted to bring me in to speak with their Board. I knew it was good, but did not want to get my hopes up as every time I did, nothing good happened. I planned to meet with them the next day and immediately let Mr. Lang know. He congratulated me and told me to call him the next day when things concluded. I said I would and that I would have Travie call him. I then called Travie and told him to contact Mr. Lang not referencing anything about my potential new position. I also encouraged him to represent himself well and if he were offered the position to work hard every day. He seemed excited and agreed. After hanging up with him my mind wandered again daydreaming about starting my own school, before I knew it it was morning and time for me to prepare for my interview. This was it; all that was standing between me and my new position was this interview. I was confident, but not cocky and knew I was going to impress them and show them that I was the right choice for their new school. As I entered I smiled, introduced myself to each Board Member, shook their hands, sat down and began to talk...

Chapter Fifty-Three

I worked to be visible in the classrooms, be accessible to them...

Going through the events of my life, my work experiences and my philosophy of education was like knowing my name, pretty easy. I saw some Board members diligently write down things I mentioned as others nodded their heads in agreement. I felt good, and then the questions started. They were nothing unexpected, but it was lengthy and overall the interview took much longer than I thought. After three hours, I was confident that I was going to get the position. They told me that they would give me a call in a few days to let me know their decision. I was proud of myself and left feeling convinced that even if I did not get the job, I had done my best and at the very least impressed them with my answers and thoughts about education.

When I returned home there was a message from Travie. He had spoken to Mr. Lang and was coming to Chicago for an interview. I did not return the call, but just sat and reflected on the events of the day. As I sat there and daydreamed about what it would be like to start my own school. The phone rang. It was the CEO letting me know that they formally wanted to offer me the position. They asked me to come in to discuss the specifics including benefits, start date and pay. I kept my cool for the conversation and once I hung up I yelled with sheer excitement. I was going to be the founding Principal of CICS Ralph Ellison on the Southside of Chicago.

After meeting with them I started my journey of recruiting staff members. I called Isaac from high school to see if he was interested in coming to work in the building. I contacted some individuals I had met through consulting and a few people I had met at conferences. I wanted my staff to be individuals I could trust and who were going to do the right thing for the population we were serving. I researched and studied the curriculum and started to piece together my vision. July 1st came faster than I had expected. We did not have our permanent building, as it was being designed and constructed. So I spent the next six weeks working to design the framework that would be the foundation for the school. Being housed in a local elementary school was not the best location, but with only freshmen it was going to be fine for the first year. The class schedule was designed; my staff and I developed discipline plans, how to meet the needs of special education students and what Ralph Ellison was going to "look like." Before I knew it registration had occurred and the first day of school had arrived.

Being a Principal was my opportunity to build long term relationships with students and families showing them the way to post secondary education, scholarships and moving towards their dreams. I knew many of my students did not have the resources or background to see beyond their present lives, as I was that way when I was younger, but I hoped to give them something I had in Coach Johnson... an adult mentor who knew their struggles, but also knew ways to move past the obstacles they faced. I worked to be visible in the classrooms, be accessible to them no matter what time or day, and know that though I was tough on them I was always fair.

Beyond being a Principal I had the chance to save a large amount of money. I worked hard to clean up my credit and put any extra money towards the stock market. By the middle of the first year at Ellison I had made enough money to start looking to buy a house. I searched hard to find something I was going to be comfortable in and gave me room to breathe. I found a nice new construction home where I could pick out the final touches and move into during the summer. As I made my way through the process, I thought back on the days of living place-to-place, sleeping on the floor, in the park and among roaches and rodents. I was embarking on the mission of providing myself a place to stay forever, and meeting the goal of never relying on someone else to put a roof over my head. I thought about Jeanie kicking me out and not having anywhere to go, seeing the orange eviction notices on the door, knowing time was running out on that dwelling and feeling worthless.

After signing the papers and receiving the key for my home, I knew I had made it. I had a good job, beautiful new house and I knew one day I would find the perfect woman to complete my puzzle. I then took the rest of my savings from the stock market and went shopping. My goal was to furnish my home with all new items within two months. By the time my second year as a Principal started my home was furnished and I was watching the stock market as I had some investments in stocks that could potentially make me a lot of money. Since I was young I wanted the basics in life and now I had achieved them. My goal with the stock market was to work towards luxuries. If I could make enough money to pay all my bills off, pay for my wants in cash and have money remaining for the proverbial rainy day, I would be well off. Little did I know in the next few months the stock market would change my life once again...

Chapter Fifty-Four

I had never seen so much money in my entire life.

Adding the second class to Ellison was a joy. I now had an additional group of students to develop relationships with. We had moved locations to a building of our own, though it was not the permanent location, which was slotted to be completed at the end of the school year for the next year. We had a pretty good idea of how things were done and though my staff was growing, I felt good about the individuals on my team and the successes we were making with our academics.

Personally, I was growing. The best thing was that Travie was now working in Chicago. I got to talk with him and see him a lot more and our relationship started to become stronger. Another great thing was that I had learned how to regularly make money in the stock market. Watching CNBC and Jim Kramer had allowed me the chance to make some additional money from my

CICS paychecks. My target was to make $10,000, which I thought was a good amount of money, and then take the profits and play with the "house money." That way I did not lose any of my own money. To my surprise, I had learned quickly, by researching and buying stocks I made my $10,000 in a week. This was too easy.

So I followed my plan. I took my money out and I was determined to use the "house money" to make more. Knowing I had nothing to lose, I spread the money among a few stocks and set my goal at $25,000. Jackpot. Six days later I had made my $25,000. This was like nothing I had ever seen before. So I set a new goal $50,000. Then $75,000. Before I knew it my goal was $100,000. I knew it was possible, but I never in a million years imagined it was going to be me. On a day off from school, I sat at my dining room table with Travie, Isaac and another friend Weave trying to explain to them the process and that they should open an account. They laughed and went to play video games. As I watched my portfolio rise, my eyes got bigger and bigger. I clicked the refresh button on the browser and with that click of the button I had $102,546 in my account. I lost my breath.

I stared at the screen. I could not smile, I could not shout, I could not laugh in excitement, just stare. I knew in the back of my mind that as fast as I made that money, I could lose it, so I hit the refresh button again. $107,876.98. I was making thousands by the second. Refresh. $113,219.41. Refresh. $127,867.70. I had to close the computer. The market was about to close and over $125,000 was sitting in my account. I could do nothing but smile. After the market closed I transferred money, went to the bank and pulled over $50,000 out of my account. I quickly drove home, went in the house, put it on the table and looked at it. Before I knew it I was like Scrooge McDuck laying in it. I had never seen so much money in my entire life. I wanted to take a picture and send it to every person who ever told me I was not going to make it. I wanted to show Travie, Ike and Weave I wanted to show Mama what hard work did. I yelled out at the top of my lungs... "I MADE IT!"

Over the next two weeks I used the money I made to pay off everything. I continued to watch the stock market and knew that I could not get too greedy. As Jim says, "Bears make money, Bulls make money and pigs get slaughtered." I just could not believe it. As I watched my portfolio climb, I eventually realized that I was being a pig and pulled every cent I had out when the account hit $167,346.78. I had always dreamed of having a BMW 745 Li so I went to go look for one. My dream was white with a tan interior. The BMW dealership had the exact car I wanted; it was like God winking at me. I purchased my car and thanked him for his blessing.

That night I went home knowing that I had made every last dream come true. I had my dream home, job, car and I did not want for anything. I was blessed. The rest of the school year went as planned. I continued to make money in the stock market. My hunger started to develop to do something more. I wanted to challenge myself with my own charter. I had started a school under someone else's idea, and now my brain stewed about being my own boss. I wanted to watch my kids graduate in two years, but I needed something else. As the bureaucracy of working in a charter school system in the Chicago public schools started to wear on me and the people running things had no true understanding of inner city youth. I knew it was time to start looking at my next journey.

Chapter Fifty-Five

55

My goal was for them to increase their scores from their initial testing,

---

Ellison was a joy to work at. The kids were fantastic, the parents were even better and watching the changes occur made me proud as a Principal. The staff was more volatile as the upper management changed frequently. They started talking to other campuses and felt the pressure to look into a union. Though my leadership had nothing to do with the need for security they moved towards unionizing three schools. There was a strong divide between doing what was right for the kids and doing what they felt was right for them. The start of the third year was fabulous and we finally were in our new state-of-the-art facility. It was beautiful.

As I went through the motions of starting a new school year, I started planning to write my own charter. Though the ideas were in my head, I struggled to put them on paper. I needed help. As the school year progressed, I started talking to a few educators in the organization and out in other districts about the idea of a new charter. Knowing that Illinois has a limited amount of available charters, getting one would be hard. However, there was a proposed legislation on the books in Springfield that might bring up the number of available charters. I wanted to have my proposal ready if the legislation passed. The more I spoke with individuals the more I knew there were two people I could work with to write the charter.

So in our free time, weekends, and nights we started planning, researching and formatting for our charter. As the charter started to come together, I had a lot at stake. My juniors were about to take the ACT. My goal was for them to increase their scores from their initial testing, when they first started at Ellison two years earlier, by 6 points. I wanted a predominantly African-American high school to surpass the National ACT average for blacks and my charter was about to be submitted to start the process of approval.

By the end of the year things were just as I wanted them. The juniors had made their score. The charter had been presented and was moving to the next stages. At this point I knew that it was time for me to leave Ellison. Though I longed to see my kids graduate, I needed to fulfill my own dream of starting my charter. Two weeks before the end of the school year I submitted my resignation, leaving to work on the development of my charter. The parents and kids were angry, sad and mad to see me go, but they all realized that there was a bigger plan for me and them.

At this point, life has taught me so many lessons. The trials and tribulations which I have experienced have shaped me as a black man. I realize Travie's words that I changed the course of the family were not only rooted in his experiences but the whole family's thoughts. Without knowing it, I created a path for the betterment of my family, through my own personal determination, desire and will. I'd like to believe they are all better because of my dream to overcome obstacles.

Travie continues to work hard in the position I helped him get. He lives around the corner from me. He has a strong loyalty to Mama, speaks with her way more often than I do, and often tries to push me to develop a better relationship with her. I love my brother and we are quite close and through the ups and downs, I know we always end up stronger.

Peanut, got into WSU and completed his bachelor's degree. He now contemplates going back for a Master's degree. Much of his time is spent with his kids. I do not have much contact with him, just like when we were younger, but I do respect his achievements and removing himself from the road he was headed down when he was younger.

I have not seen nor spoken to Junior in many years. I probably would not know him if I walked next to him on the street. Though Mama maintains contact with him, there is really nothing I have to say to him. The same situation goes for Jeanie. I do not want to see her or need to ever see her again. She was not a positive influence on my life, but on the other hand she motivated me to be more than she ever could dream of. Overall, her existence means nothing to me.

Benny divorced Sharon and started his life over, clean. He remains in LA, but now works hard to pay bills, keep food on the table and provide for his new wife. He is nearing retirement and out of everyone, I feel most connected to him. When I was younger I never would have believed it, but we are a lot alike. He likes to be by himself and does not reach out a lot. He is comfortable in his circle and does not let many people in. We talk regularly and as I get older I can appreciate his words and understanding of life. I have learned to respect him for the journey he has traveled and the lessons he has acquired along the way.

My relationship with Mama is one that goes up and down. She is clean now and even went back to complete her GED as well as graduated with an associate's degree. Though she has achieved these accomplishments, she does not have a full time job. She now resides in Texas and regularly calls me to talk about this and that, trying to build a new relationship with me. Understanding her mentality, I take it for what it is and appreciate having my mother still around as her health has deteriorated over the years. I cannot say we are close, but I can say that I try to build bridges with her and hopefully over time, we will have some type of understanding.

There is not a day that goes by that I do not think about Bernard. I know he is my angel. He watches over me and I work to make him proud. It pains me to think that he is not here with me, but I know he is in a better place. I have to believe that. I have accepted that his mission is to be my guardian angel and he works hard at his mission. I would not have made it without him. While here on Earth he was my support, guide and strength, and now that he is in heaven. He remains those things to me. I know one day we will meet again, but until that day I thank him for his words of encouragement the day I left. I will never forget his voice or what he said, that has made me what I am today.

Growing up I never knew how powerful the mind could be. I strongly believe that the mind can control your perceptions.

It controls whether you are an optimist or pessimist. It controls how you view adversity – whether you let them hold you down or use them as stepping stones of motivation. Your mind dictates how you view life and whether you feel like you are in control or if life is controlling you. My mind told me that I had a responsibility to myself to do what others told me I could not do. So many people get stuck in the norms of survival rather than adapt to situations using them to propel themselves out. I was almost stuck in what would have been an easy choice to make. Instead I used my struggles as motivation. Now I want others to do the same.

The 'hood is like a waterfall. When living there, you are faced with endless problems and limited solutions. When you think you have found a way out of the roughest of situations, the problems keep pouring down from above. You always can breathe enough to stay alive, but as the water keeps falling, you slowly begin to drown. Eventually your breath will give up and your heart will stop. I almost stopped breathing, but I was given the chance to see beyond the waterfall. I was given the hope of more than just enough breath. I was given the breath of hope. I saw that with hard work I could escape the waterfall and have what I dreamt of.

Growing up I experienced a great number of obstacles. I know what it feels like to have people laugh at you because you have nothing. I know what it feels like to have nowhere to live, nothing to eat, parents who do not care about you, feel dumb and understand your life is nothing but a ticking time bomb waiting to explode. But I used that to fuel my fire and stubbornness to work harder and longer for more. Below are 10 tips that I have developed through my life to keep me reaching for my dreams:

1. Know there is always someone to believe in you. If you believe there is no one there, look in the mirror and believe in yourself. That is really all you need.
2. Understand that personal perseverance is the way to push through even the toughest challenges.
3. The obstacles and hard times you face are put there for one of two reasons – to either make you stronger or to make you weaker. Use them to make you stronger.
4. Education is something that no one can ever take from you. The more knowledge you have the better off you are. Never neglect your mind, its power and its potential.
5. Experience things outside your daily life, neighborhood and community. There are a world of opportunities, chances, experiences and dreams out there for you to seek. If you continue to stay where you live, you will continue to get what you have always gotten. Branch out and use the world as your resource.
6. Standing still is very different than still standing.
7. Anything is possible. Once you open your mind, you can gain complete control over how you interpret the world.
8. Keep your friends close, learn from your enemies, and understand that nothing lasts forever. Through your trials and tribulations, keep your head up, pain is temporary and misery is optional.
9. If you are doing what you are supposed to be doing, don't be surprised that you will have haters. The more haters you have, the more you are doing right.
10. Remember you were put here to complete an assignment. The assignment is always bigger than you. Work hard to complete that assignment to the best of your ability and never let anyone deter you from your work.

The lessons I have come to understand are best summed up in understanding my assignment is to work to help children overcome the issues they have encountered. I am an example that anything is possible. I had a number of enemies (drugs, gangs, family, poverty, homelessness, special education, behavior, anger... the list goes on and on) growing up and now I see that the enemies I had did not fight me for where I was but they were fighting me for where I was going. I have learned that my heredity was not my destiny. When I was young I let others put doubt in my mind about what I was going to be, what I could do and what I could not do. Now I know that I am (as you are) a seed of greatness, a person of destiny, and I should not let anyone put doubt in my mind (as you should not let others put doubt in your mind). I have learned that people like Junior and Jeanie were put in my life to motivate me. The more they talked, the more I was graced with stones to step over obstacles. They wanted to see me fail. They wanted to be able to say that I was no better than them, but instead their wicked desires became my blessings. I have to believe that I was blessed by the angels (like Bernard) watching over me. I knew that where I was, was not where I was staying and the blessings granted to me were there to move me on.

I hope that this story is one of hope. I hope that I have been your blessing to see that your life is more than you ever imagined it could be. Use that as your motivation. Use your education as a tool to sculpt your dreams and complete your goals. Anything is possible, but nothing comes easy. Hard work is what separates the ordinary from the extraordinary. You too can break the cycle and become everything you know you can become. The only person who can control your future is the person you look at every day in the mirror. Be designed to embrace beyond what you see, but instead accept what you envision. Refuse to settle for what is given to you and create a path of your own destiny. Do not be the puppet of others, but be the puppet master of yourself.

I have become my own puppet master. I now work towards

opening my charter and hope to guide urban youth to a brighter future. I want children to have paths full of choices. I want them to understand and use the power of education, perseverance, hard work, visualization, the words of others, but most of all the power of their dreams. I want each urban child to be better than what they have seen in the 'hood and embark on new journeys beyond their neighborhoods. Know that your future is in your hands and complete the assignment you were put here to complete to the best of your ability. I hope that my story and words inspire you to reflect on your own future and institute your own positive self fulfilling prophecy, just like my reflection has done for me.

Dear Children,

I wish to acknowledge you, the thousands and thousands of innocent ghetto kids suffering every day from a life you do not deserve to live. I want you to know that I understand your sufferings; I have been where you are today. I want you to know that I wrote this book for you. I wanted everyone to hear your cries and to understand the pain you face. I wanted you, the suffering youth, to understand that you are trained to become what you see everyday. You are trained to be thugs. You are designed to accept what you were born into, and at the same time, you are being persuaded to think that this is the right way to live. The people in your life all play a role in how you view it: Your friends, your environment, the adults in your life, the media, and even your own thought process. Your society is designed to keep you in the dark.

The life you are living right now is not the life you have to live forever. The anger you feel in your heart is not the anger you are supposed to feel for the rest of your life. You are programmed to think this way; you are influenced to believe your skin is a sin. You are trained to look at each other as if you were without value, so you talk to each other with disrespect, you kill each other out of ignorance and give up on life because you are taught not to be persistent. We, who live in the bellows of urban America, are taught to embrace its mentality. What is the ghetto mentality? It is a mentality that does not define you as a person, but a mentality that defines your position in life.

My children, you are programmed to give up on life. You are programmed since birth to believe that ghetto kids don't need education because they won't live long enough to use it. Although you don't realize it now, every interaction you have in life, whether it's positive or negative, stays in your brain and in your thought process forever. When you hear people talk about killing, you become numb to it. You don't look at it as a big deal. When you see people who look like you selling dope, you become numb to it. When those around you don't embrace school and knowledge, you begin subconsciously to fall into the norm as well, believing that it's not a big deal. And before you know it, your life has slipped away and you begin to fall into the ghetto norm. You feel that this is your life and that you must simply deal with it. This is your negative self fulfilling prophecy.

I am here to let you know that the information that has been fed to you since birth is a lie. Don't believe it. Trust me, I know. You can become a doctor, a lawyer, a teacher, a scientist – anything you desire. You have a brain just like any other human being in the world; how you use it determines your individuality. How you see your future, determines your future. Your positive thoughts become your positive self fulfilling prophecy. You are not destined to fail; you are destined to prevail. You are not destined to be a thug; you are destined to grow and blossom so that you can show love to your child. You are not destined to live a short life, but you are destined to gain knowledge and overcome the miserable conditions you were dealt at first light.

I want to acknowledge you, the unblossomed seed – the seed that is not being nurtured and constantly bleeds. I want to shine the light on you, the beautiful child who can see it through. I want to water you with love, so that you grow and blossom from below. You and I together, we all can be free. Not free in the physical sense, but free within our minds, because through them, the purest light can shine.

- Doc

FROM SPECIAL ED. TO PH.D

The liberation process of a man named Eboni
From the pits of the ghetto,
to the land that's mellow
I rose

Through the hunger and pain.
I found a way to gain
I rose

From begging for money, because my
mother wouldn't put food in my tummy
I rose

From pumping gas to get some
hard earned cash
I rose

I fought through the adversity,
and refuse to submit with mercy
I rose

From the confinement of the ghetto's gate,
I emerged away from the hate
I rose

From losing a brother, and having a
crack head for a mother
I rose

*From having a burden of a crack
addicted father, a man who never really
seemed to bother
I rose*

*I battled, and won the war of poverty,
I defied the odds on my society
From sole-less shoes, and inner-city blues
I rose*

*I refused to submit to the lies and deceit,
because I recognized the trap that was
designed for me
I rose*

*From the crack cocaine that destroyed
my family, that powerful substance,
that kills you rapidly
I rose*

*From my grave, I recognized the facade,
and chose a new path to pave
I rose*

*I journeyed to that distant place,
unaware of my fate, yet overwhelmed
with joy, cause I now can liberate
I rose*

From the stereotype that was placed on me, the illusion that I could see clearly, because I yearned to be free
I rose

I've reached the place that many would cherish, I shocked those who thought my dreams would perish
I rose

It took me 24 years to finally get here, now I can breathe because I no longer have to live in fear
I rose